PETER'S PEOPLE,
THE OUTRAGEOUS NEW BOOK
BY THE AUTHOR OF
THE PETER PRINCIPLE,
THE MULTI-MILLION-COPY BESTSELLER
THAT PEOPLE WILL BE TALKING ABOUT
AS LONG AS THINGS GO WRONG!

Praise for
The Peter Principle

"Stimulating, amusing reading . . ."
—*Book World*

"As funny a book as has come along in a long
while . . . brilliant."
—*Chicago Sun-Times*

"A hilarious piece of work."
—*National Observer*

"Read this book and grow wise."
—*Associated Press*

"Ruefully delightful . . . excruciatingly applicable—
and fun to read!"
—*Playboy*

"A cultural phenomenon . . . its title phrase is certain
to enter the language."
—*Life*

Books by Laurence J. Peter

PETER'S PEOPLE
PETER'S QUOTATIONS
THE PETER PLAN
INDIVIDUAL INSTRUCTION
CLASSROOM INSTRUCTION
THERAPEUTIC INSTRUCTION
TEACHER EDUCATION
THE PETER PRESCRIPTION
THE PETER PRINCIPLE (*WITH RAYMOND HULL*)
PRESCRIPTIVE TEACHING

PETER'S PEOPLE

BY

Dr. Laurence J. Peter

Illustrated by Matt Wuerker

TOWER BOOKS NEW YORK CITY

A TOWER BOOK

Published by

Tower Publications, Inc.
Two Park Avenue
New York, N.Y. 10016

Copyright ©MCMLXXIX by Laurence J. Peter

Published by arrangement with
William Morrow & Company, Inc.

TO

MARSHALL LUMSDEN in appreciation of his part in the development of this work. As editor of *Human Behavior* magazine he requested that I write the column "Peter's People" that became the basis for this book. In doing this he was repeating his earlier involvement that changed my life dramatically. In 1967, as editor for the *Los Angeles Times West* magazine, he commissioned me to write an article about the Peter Principle. It was this article that aroused the interest of publishers in *The Peter Principle*, thus ending years of futile effort to get the book published. I gratefully acknowledge the catalytic role he played in my writing career.

CONTENTS

PETER'S
PEOPLE

Introduction

THIS IS A BOOK ABOUT PEOPLE AND THEIR IDEAS. ALL THE people stories are brief, and most of the ideas are expressed in epigrammatic form. This succinct way of writing had its origins in my childhood, when I started a hobby that is with me to this day. I began collecting quotations. Some favorite early entries in my first scrapbook were:

I am free of all prejudices. I hate everybody equally.
—W. C. FIELDS

My heart is as pure as the driven slush.
—TALLULAH BANKHEAD

Life is like an onion: you peel it off one layer at a time and sometimes you weep.
—CARL SANDBURG

Never put off till tomorrow what you can do the day after tomorrow.

—MARK TWAIN

As the years passed, I became increasingly fascinated by wise and witty ideas expressed in a few words of pithy prose. During my early years of quotemongering I accumulated gems of distilled thought simply for the pleasure of possessing words and ideas that sparkled. In the process I acquired a veritable idea mine in which prospecting was a rewarding experience.

When I became a writer, my collecting hobby paid off in unexpected ways. I discovered that I was emulating the authors of my favorite quotes by having something to say and saying what I wanted to say in as few words as possible. As I studied the works of these admired writers, I found that language is used for two purposes: (1) to convey information, as in "I'll have a corned beef on rye" or "Mary had a little lamb, its fleece was white as snow" and (2) to establish order in a chaotic world, as in the Chinese proverbs "No matter how deep you dig your well, it affords poor refuge in times of flood" or "Only the brave deserve the fair, but only the fat, rich, cowardly merchant can afford same."

I used the first type of language when writing about people. This applied whether I was writing about individuals such as George Carlin or Adlai Stevenson or groups of people such as writers or politicians. The second type of language is used in writing axioms, epigrams, hypotheses, rules, theories, proverbs, laws, and principles. For convenience I include all these one-liners, which attempt to make sense of the human condition, under the general title of "laws." Therefore, Acton's Rule, Murphy's Law, and Peter's Principle are all referred to as laws, although these titles suggest subtle differences of meaning. You will find laws throughout the book and a final chapter devoted entirely to the subject.

Some of the people populating this book are little known, some are well known, some are celebrities; but each is here because of what he or she said or did or wrote. None is here only because of his or her fame.

Ours is the age of the media-created celebrity—the age of publicity where we are fed prefabricated opinions about who should receive our attention. Heroes or persons of real accomplishment have long since been replaced by images created by public relations departments. The hero of days gone by was known for having done something; the celebrity of today is known for being known.

Each person herein represents unique accomplishment. You may regard that accomplishment as heroic, trivial, or despicable, but you will find reading about it entertaining.

There is no attempt in these word sketches to provide well-rounded pictures or condensed biographies. Each character study has a point of view and essentially explores just one characteristic or area of accomplishment of each person. The P. T. Barnum story shows his influence on American history. His personal problems and failed business ventures, interesting though they be to biographers, were deemed irrelevant to the purpose of this book. Will Rogers's facility with satire was central, so the piece directs attention to his humorous but profound remarks and omits reference to his broad interests and many charitable activities. The Johnny Carson article explores his place in the history of American entertainment but provides none of the items of gossip that form the basis of much writing about entertainers.

An old friend of mine used to put me on the spot by asking, "Now, Peter, tell me honestly, as an outsider, what do you think of the human race?" It was a difficult question, but at least, when writing this book, I am not an outsider. This is the most personal writing for publication I have done. Ostensibly a book about other people, it is actually about me and is the closest to being an autobiography that I ever intend to write. Like you, in large measure I am what I am because of how I relate to others and how they relate to me and how I respond to their ideas and they respond to mine. So here I am with people, alive and dead, who aroused my interest or admiration and who, above all, wrought changes in my thinking and my life.

ACKNOWLEDGMENTS

Many of the articles about people first appeared in *Human Behavior* magazine between July 1976 and May 1979 under the title "Peter's People." The article "Was Nixon a Victim of the Peter Principle?" first appeared as a public service message, sponsored by Bernard Rapoport, in *The Texas Observer*, December 13, 1974, and the research report "Selecting a School Counselor" was first published by *The Clearing House*, October 1964.

CHAPTER 1

The Pen Is Mightier

MORE THAN A HUNDRED YEARS AGO EDWARD BULWER-LYTTON wrote, "The pen is mightier than the sword." In the light of history it is a pretty silly statement. Logan Pearsall Smith described it as a "perfectly appalling statement," and Miguel de Cervantes said, "Let none presume to tell me that the pen is preferable to the sword." Oscar Wilde wrote, "It was a fatal day when the public discovered that the pen is mightier than the paving stone, and can be made as offensive as the brick-bat." He also said, "One dagger will do more than a hundred epigrams." Obviously the pen is not mightier than the sword, but it must be mightier than something. The more I think about it, the more I am inclined to dismiss the whole idea. It was written by a writer, not a swordsman, and is probably just a self-serving statement.

My favorite interpretation was made by Marvin Kitman when he said that it was intended to show the desirability of a prescription over surgery.

In the contest between writing and killing, one thing seems clear: The pen is funnier than the sword.

WILDE KINGDOM

The story of Oscar Wilde's life has been the subject of numerous books—and what a life. Until he was forty, his life was a masterpiece of creativity and witty, gorgeous elegance.

He was born in Dublin on October 16, 1854. His father was a doctor, and his mother a poet and Irish patriot. Oscar

attended Dublin's Trinity College, then Magdalen College, Oxford. He gained a reputation as a dandy and wit; his dress, manners, and speech were impeccable. When ridiculed for his lack of naturalness, he replied, "To be natural is such a very difficult pose to keep up."

His literary gifts were recognized early, and in 1878 he was awarded a Double First in Classical Moderation and Humane Letters. He also won the Newdigate Prize for Poetry.

In 1884 he married Constance Lloyd, by whom he had two sons. During the next few years, while editing a monthly called the *Woman's World* and writing literary notes for that publication, he also gained success as the author of *The Picture of Dorian Gray, Lord Arthur Savile's Crime, and Other Stories, A House of Pomegranates, Intentions,* and a tract on *The Soul of Man Under Socialism.* His plays, *Lady Windermere's Fan, A Woman of No Importance,* and *The*

Importance of Being Earnest, were great theatrical successes
in London.

It was while touring America at the age of twenty-six that
he discovered his bisexuality, which, once recognized, he
could not suppress. His sexual tastes and habits exposed him
to blackmail and disgrace. In an attempt to halt his accusers
he sued for libel, but the evidence introduced at the trial led
to criminal proceedings against him. He went to prison for
two years. In 1897 he went to Paris, where he wrote *The
Ballad of Reading Gaol* and *De Profundis*.

Because Wilde died in Paris on November 30, 1900, all
his answers to my questions are taken verbatim from his
writings or from the published record of his conversations.[1]

PETER: It is a rare privilege to meet you.

WILDE: Oh, I'm so glad you've come. There are a hundred
things I want not to say to you.

PETER: I am here to interview you for *Human Behavior*
magazine.

WILDE: Journalism justifies its own existence by the great
Darwinian principle of the survival of the vulgarest.

PETER: Doing this is just a hobby. I am the author of *The
Peter Principle* and other books.

WILDE: I don't like principles . . . I prefer prejudices. I
hate people who talk about themselves, as you do, when
one wants to talk about oneself, as I do.

PETER: I'm sorry. I was just trying to explain. . . .

WILDE: I rely on you to misrepresent me.

PETER: I thought you wanted this press coverage.

WILDE: In the old days men had the rack, now they have
the Press.

PETER: You seem upset. Are you ill?

WILDE: No, not ill, but very weary. The fact is I picked a
primrose in the wood yesterday, and it was so ill that I
have been sitting up with it all night.

PETER: I hope you will find my questions worthwhile.

WILDE: It is always worth while asking a question, though it is not always worth while answering one.

PETER: Before we get to discussing your work, I'd like to ask a few personal questions. What is your reaction to the scandal surrounding your life?

WILDE: I love scandals about other people, but scandals about myself don't interest me. They have not got the charm of novelty.

PETER: Has it hurt your status as an author?

WILDE: A good reputation is one of the many annoyances to which I have never been subjected. There is only one thing in the world worse than being talked about, and that is not being talked about. A man who is much talked about is always attractive. One feels there must be something in him, after all. If your sins find you out, why worry! It is when they find you in, that trouble begins. I don't at all like knowing what people say of me behind my back. It makes one far too conceited.

PETER: You don't regard your reputation seriously?

WILDE: Life is much too important a thing ever to talk seriously about it. I sometimes think that God in creating man, somewhat overestimated His ability.

PETER: But you must have some serious thoughts about life.

WILDE: Have I not stood face to face with beauty, that is enough for one man's life. We can have in life but one great experience at best, and the secret of life is to reproduce that experience as often as possible. To live is the rarest thing in the world. Most people exist, that is all. One can survive everything nowadays, except death, and live down anything except a good reputation. Moods don't last. It is their chief charm.

PETER: That's beautiful!

WILDE: When people agree with me I always feel that I must be wrong.

PETER: You have earned an undisputed placē in English literature with works that are completely dissimilar in character. You predicted this back in your days at Oxford when you said, "I'll be a poet, a writer, a dramatist. Somehow or other I'll be famous. I'll be notorious."

WILDE: To love oneself is the beginning of a life-long romance.

PETER: After all these years, how do you feel about your most popular work, *The Importance of Being Earnest*?

WILDE: The first act is ingenious, the second beautiful, the third abominably clever.

PETER: What is your motivation for writing?

WILDE: I write because it gives me the greatest possible artistic pleasure to write. All fine imaginative work is self-conscious and deliberate. No poet sings because he must sing. At least no great poet does. A great poet sings because he chooses to sing.

PETER: You have been criticized for writing immoral books.

WILDE: There is no such thing as a moral or an immoral book. Books are well written or badly written. That is all. The popular novel that the public calls healthy is always a thoroughly unhealthy production; and what the public calls an unhealthy novel is always a beautiful and healthy work of art. The books that the world calls immoral books are books that show the world its own shame.

PETER: Do we need to be reminded?

WILDE: Vulgarity and stupidity are two very vivid facts in modern life. One regrets them naturally. But there they are. The best that one can say of most modern creative art is that it is just a little less vulgar than reality.

PETER: Can you tell us something about the way you go about the task of writing?

WILDE: I was working on the proof of one of my poems all morning and took out a comma. In the afternoon I put it back again. I never put off till tomorrow what I can possibly do—the day after.

PETER: What is your own favorite reading?

WILDE: I never travel without my diary. One should always have something sensational to read in the train.

PETER: How do you feel about other modern writers?

WILDE: The ancient historians gave us delightful fiction in the form of fact; the modern novelist presents us with dull facts under the guise of fiction.

PETER: You have said some unkind things about the works of Charles Dickens.

WILDE: One must have a heart of stone to read the death of Little Nell without laughing.

PETER: You criticize Dickens for being a propagandist for social change, yet you yourself oppose war.

WILDE: As long as war is regarded as wicked, it will always have its fascination. When it is looked upon as vulgar it will cease to be popular.

PETER: As the recognized spokesman for the aesthetic movement advocating art for art's sake you seem to resent authority in any form.

WILDE: All authority is quite degrading. It degrades those who exercise it, and it degrades those over whom it is exercised. People sometimes enquire what form of government is most suitable for an artist to live under. To this question there is only one answer. The form of government that is most suitable to the artist is no government at all. High hopes were once formed of democracy; but democracy means simply the bludgeoning of the people by the people for the people.

PETER: And your views on religion . . .

WILDE: Religion is the fashionable substitute for Belief. Religions die when they are proved to be true. Science is the record of dead religions.

PETER: What do you believe in?

WILDE: The true artist is a man who believes absolutely in himself, because he is absolutely himself.

PETER: Is that why great writers don't get along together?

WILDE: Geniuses . . . are always talking about themselves when I want them to be thinking about me.

PETER: In closing, I am sure that my readers would be interested to know if you have any formulas for your remarkably good health.

WILDE: I am afraid I play no outdoor games at all, except dominoes. . . . I have sometimes played dominoes outside French cafés. I have made an important discovery . . . that alcohol, taken in sufficient quantities, produces all the effects of intoxication. I can resist everything except temptation.

PETER: I never know when to take you seriously.

WILDE: I am sure you must have a great future in literature before you . . . because you seem to be such a very bad interviewer. I feel sure that you must write poetry. I certainly like the colour of your necktie very much. Goodbye.

A LOVER OF WORDS

Mr. Land was taking a photograph of his daughter. After he snapped the shutter of his conventional camera, she asked, "Where is the picture?" It took him some time to answer, but when he did, he had invented the Polaroid camera. It would be interesting to know, today, how much Edwin Land of Polaroid Corporation values his daughter's question. I suspect that in reflective moments his thoughts go back to that incident and how an apparently innocent question changed his life and indirectly the whole business of photography.

What I do know is that often, while writing, I pause and in a meditative mood reflect on the events that brought me from a career in education and psychology to that of author. One such chance happening stands out as the initiating event.

Back in the fifties, while at graduate school at Western Washington State University in Bellingham, I attended a lec-

Armour Vincit Omnia

ture by the American humorist, essayist, satirist, and light versifier Richard Armour.* At that time I knew little about him except that I was an ardent fan of his light verse that appeared regularly in the *Saturday Evening Post*. I had collected such classics as:

---

* Today, at seventy-two years of age, Richard Armour keeps up a hectic pace of writing, lecturing, and teaching. He has more than 6,000 published poems and thousands of published essays and short quips to his credit. Recently he published his fifty-fifth book, of light verse and prose, for children and adults, on subjects ranging from dinosaurs to a history of art. He believes that the satirist is often misunderstood, in that the public is inclined to think he dislikes what he satirizes. Just the opposite is true. Armour's favorite subjects for humor are women, marriage, and wives. He makes fun of them because he knows them best, and to know them is to love and respect their wonderful oddities and inconsistencies. He has known his beautiful wife, Kathleen, since they were together in first grade and is enthusiastic about their marriage. So naturally that quirk of mind known as the satirical muse would seek women, marriage, and wives as subjects for its jesting.

Lady Shoppers, Beware

Show-window manikins
Have slender fannykins.

Willing Workers

People with an axe to grind,
  Much as we deplore them,
Are no worse than those we find
  Turning grindstones for them.

The auditorium was packed. The heavyset aging president
of the university made his way slowly to the podium and
began the introduction. He spoke of Dr. Armour's Harvard
Ph.D. in English philology, his various appointments as dis-
tinguished professor of English literature at universities from
Germany to Hawaii, and his scholarly volumes of literary
biography. The introduction had me expecting the worst. Then
a slim man, with an impressive bald head, stepped quickly
to the podium and addressed the audience: "You were expecting a longhair—not a no-hair!" He proceeded to deliver
his lecture in a lively, entertaining, and completely nonprofes-
sorial manner. When illustrating various points about writing,
he read from his own works with the timing of an accomplished actor.

Middle Age

Middle age
Is a time of life
A man first notices
In his wife.

Philosophy of a Late Riser

Day breaks, it's said,
  When night is ended.

I stay in bed
  Until it's mended.

Going to Extremes

Shake and shake
    The catsup bottle.
None will come
    And then a lot'll.

He read excerpts from his satirical versions of history. His samples of *It All Started with Columbus* [2] were loaded with the verbal mischief and wordplay that are characteristic of the Armour style. In *It All Started with Eve,* [3] he exposed the folly of the widely held male belief that there are fewer women who are too beautiful than women who aren't beautiful enough.

He cited the example of Helen of Troy, who was, like others, a beautiful baby. She was an exception even in Greece, for while she started out beautiful, she kept improving. By the time she was ten, men were carried away by her beauty, and she was carried away by an Athenian named Theseus. Thus began an adventure that led to her marriage with the king of Sparta. She did not become Helen of Sparta, though, because Paris later took her to Troy and married her. This resulted in Sparta's building a thousand ships for an attack on Troy. That was the beginning of the saying "The face that launched a thousand ships." The Greeks won the war in ten years, and the king took Helen back to Sparta. The trip took eight years, but getting there was half the fun. Thousands of Greeks and Trojans had been killed because, Armour claims, Helen had "the fatal gift of beauty." He concluded, "Beauty is only skin deep, and the world is full of thin-skinned people."

What impressed me most was Armour's way with serious issues. Through satire he was able to shed new light on current events.

Hiding Place

A speaker at a meeting of the New York State Frozen Food Locker Association declared that the best hiding place in event of an atomic explosion is a frozen-food locker, where "radiation will not penetrate" (news item).

> Move over, ham
>   And quartered cow,
> My Geiger says
>   The time is now.
>
> Yes, now I lay me
>   Down to sleep,
> And if I die,
>   At least I'll keep.

One use of satire is to debunk the bunk that "experts" try to dump on us and to deflate the overinflated. Another use of satire is to express serious concerns in entertaining ways. Prior to the time of that lecture, I had been studying (1) the personality dynamics of school counselors and (2) the personnel promotion procedures used within a public school system. My attempts to communicate the results of my studies had been generally ignored. I decided right then and there to try satire as the means of spreading my message. My first published satire was *Selecting a School Counselor* (see Chapter 2). I later wrote my promotional studies as *The Peter Principle* (see Chapter 8). Thanks to Armour's inspiration, here I am today, living it up in beautiful Southern California, leading the soft life of a writer.

ABE MARTIN SPEAKS

It has been said that Frank McKinney "Kin" Hubbard made more money at the trade of writing than any other American. I have been unable to verify this, but he probably was paid more per word than anyone else.

His daily newspaper feature started as a cartoon of a character called Abe Martin. Abe Martin was a cracker-barrel philosopher who observed human caprice and commented

upon it. Kin Hubbard invested Abe Martin with abundant perspicacity. From his seat on a rail fence Abe saw what was going on and described it in a few well-chosen words.

Beauty is only skin deep, but it's a valuable asset if you're poor or haven't any sense.

Abe Martin's ability to spot the main point and express it in one sentence led Kin Hubbard to write one of the shortest newspaper features on record. It was called "Abe Martin Says" and consisted of just two unrelated sentences.

The fellow who owns his own home is always just coming out of a hardware store.
Being an optimist after you've got everything you want doesn't count.

Originally his pair of one-liners appeared in the Indianapolis *News*, which gained him great readership throughout Indiana. In 1910 another Hoosier, George Ade, a nationally famous humorist, wrote about Kin, and this started the spread of his popularity throughout the country. Eventually his column was syndicated in 200 newspapers. Some papers with large circulations paid as much as $50 a day in order to publish those two sentences. The result was that his income was tremendous for that time. Kin said, "I was making more money than I had ever supposed there was." When he died in 1930, at the age of sixty-two, a nation mourned. He received an unprecedented tribute. His funeral service was the first to be broadcast over a radio network.

The charm of Kin Hubbard's apparently simple remarks cannot easily be explained. He had a gift for saying common things in an uncommon way. "The bee isn't really that busy— it just can't buzz any slower." He also had a way of telling a story, leaving the details to the reader.

> Miss Linnet Spry was confined to her home with a swollen dresser drawer.
> When Lem Moon was acquitted for the murder of his wife and Judge Pusey asked him if he had anything to say, he replied: "I never would have shot her if I'd know'd I'd have to go through so much red tape."
> Mrs. Lafe Bud's grandfather passed away yesterday. He had long been prominent in the business life of the community and was a constant church-goer till he got a car.*

Kin had Abe Martin say, "What this country needs is a good five-cent cigar." Later this saying was picked up by Tom Marshall, Vice-President of the United States, and thus, it entered our folklore. The surrealistic quality of this and other of Kin's lines may be the secret of their appeal.

> There's nothing a vulture hates more than biting into a glass eye.
> It's almost got so you can't speak the truth without committing an indiscretion.

* Kin Hubbard, in the tradition of popular writers of the past, such as Josh Billings and Artemus Ward, wrote in rural dialect. "He sayed 'e shood meet me 'n too daze 'n Kaliforny wi' enuff o' this ere jerkt befe, salt, 'n vittles, etsettery." To make it easier for the modern reader not accustomed to this style, I have used standard spelling for some of the words that were originally written in dialect.

I often wonder if the money a mother saves by cutting her boy's hair ever does her any good.

He made some astute observations about human behavior.

There isn't much to be seen in a little town, but what you hear makes up for it.

It's purty hard to be efficient without being obnoxious.

When a feller says, "It ain't the money, but the principle of the thing," it's the money.

A never failing way to get rid of a feller is to tell him something for his own good.

If there's anything a public servant hates to do it's something for the public.

Very often the quiet feller has said all he knows.

Some fellers are too polite to be up to any good.

It's no disgrace to be poor but it might as well be.

The feller that agrees with everything you say is either a fool or he is getting ready to skin you.

His view of politics was consistently antagonistic.

If the Government was as afraid of disturbing the consumer as it is of disturbing business, this would be some democracy.

A diplomat is a feller that lets you do all the talking while he gets what he wants.

It seems like nothing ever gets to going good till there's a few resignations.

It seems like the less a statesman amounts to the more he loves the flag.

Now and then an innocent man is sent to the legislature.

Some fellers get credit for being conservative when they're only stupid.

There's very little discussion of either peace or war down our way, except by folks who talk too blamed much on any subject.

If there's any literary ability in a feller, getting fired out of a good government job will bring it out.

He had no difficulty in expressing his ideas about love, marriage, and raising children.

The feller who waits to get married until he has enough money isn't really in love.

I never remember whether a pleasant woman was pretty or not.

The man who eats his breakfast downtown often stays late at the office.

Tipton Bud has got a joke on his wife. She thinks he's losing his hearing.

Nobody works as hard for his money as the man who marries it.

"We just can't agree," said Lafe Bud, in referring to his divorce suit, "and when we do agree we're both wrong."

"Well, sir, it was the best I could do at the time," said ole Dan Moss, when asked how in the world he happened to marry his uncle's widow.

The reason parents no longer lead their children in the right direction is because the parents aren't going that way themselves.

Most parents don't worry about a daughter until she fails to show up for breakfast.

The worst waste of breath, next to playing a saxophone, is advising a son.

We like little children because they tear out as soon as they get what they want.

His comments on life covered a wide range of subjects.

Miss Germ Williams is just a natural-born artist and draws portraits on ruled paper so she can keep the ears even.

Classic music is the kind that we keep thinking will turn into a tune.

If at first you do succeed, don't take any more chances.

Intelligent people are always on the unpopular side of anything.

I'll bet the hardest thing about prizefighting is picking up your teeth with a boxing glove on.

It ain't a bad plan to keep still occasionally even when you know what you're talking about.

A restaurant waiter always lays your check on the table upside down so you won't choke to death.

A grouch escapes so many little annoyances that it almost pays to be one.

No one can feel as helpless as the owner of a sick goldfish.

The reason the way of the transgressor is hard is because it's so crowded.

Another good thing about the movie theater is that there's no encores.

It's kind of fun these days just to plug along and wonder what you're going to get stung on next.

It must be great to be rich and let the other fellow keep up appearances.

We're all pretty much alike when we get out of town.

An optimist is a feller who believes what's going to be will be postponed.

MOST OF THEM NEVER HAPPENED

Samuel Langhorne Clemens was born on November 30, 1835, in Florida, Missouri, and grew up along the banks of the Mississippi. He spent almost half his life as a wanderer, newspaper reporter, and worker at odd jobs. For more than three years he plied the Mississippi River as a steamboat apprentice and became a licensed pilot in 1859. In 1861 he traveled west to write and in 1863 adopted the pen name Mark Twain. As Mark Twain, his humorous stories and lectures made him famous, but in 1891 he became embroiled in financial problems and moved to Europe. Solvent again in 1900, he returned to America, where he was in great demand as a speaker. He was such a crowd pleaser that he became, in competition with singers, dancers, instrumentalists, and actors, one of the most popular performers of his time. For one of the great writers of all time to be also one of the great entertainers was unique. Because in his lectures and in his writing his ambition was to sweep away superstition, prejudice, and illusion, his message is still valid. He died on April 21, 1910, in Redding, Connecticut, so his answers to my questions are all statements he made during his lifetime.

PETER: It gives me great pleasure to find you looking so young and fit.

TWAIN: When your friends begin to flatter you on how young you look, it's a sure sign you're getting old.

PETER: Now that your books have become so popular, do you think they will become classics?

TWAIN: A classic is something that everybody wants to have read and nobody wants to read.

PETER: You have written both fiction and nonfiction. Which do you find more interesting?

TWAIN: Truth is stranger than fiction, but it is because fiction is obliged to stick to possibilities: truth isn't.

PETER: Why are you so critical of your fellowman?

TWAIN: Man is the creature made at the end of the week's work when God was tired.

PETER: Isn't that an overly harsh view of humanity?

TWAIN: Such is the human race. Often it does seem such a pity that Noah . . . didn't miss the boat.

PETER: But hasn't man progressed ethically?

TWAIN: An ethical man is a Christian holding four aces.

PETER: But he has a conscience.

TWAIN: Man is the only animal that blushes. Or needs to.

PETER: Well, if man is so hopeless, why do you urge him to be good?

TWAIN: To be good is noble, but to teach others how to be good is nobler—and less trouble.

PETER: You have expressed many original ideas in your writing.

TWAIN: Adam was the only man who, when he said a good thing, knew that nobody had said it before him.

PETER: On one hand, you seem to admire technological progress, and on the other, you write fondly of the uneducated views of Huckleberry Finn.

TWAIN: We have not the reverent feeling for the rainbow that the savage has, because we know how it is made. We have lost as much as we gained by prying into that matter.

PETER: Do you have disdain for formal education?

TWAIN: I have never let my schooling interfere with my education.

PETER: Why are you so critical of so many educated men?

TWAIN: The man who does not read good books has no advantage over the man who can't read them.

PETER: Why do you think our schools fail?

TWAIN: In the first place God made idiots. This was for practice. Then he made school boards.

PETER: Do you believe that one learns more through experience?

TWAIN: We should be careful to get out of an experience only the wisdom that is in it—and stop there; lest we be like the cat that sits down on a hot stove-lid. She will never sit down on a hot stove-lid again—and that is well; but also she will never sit down on a cold one anymore.

PETER: To what do you credit America's success?

TWAIN: It is by the goodness of God that in our country we have those three unspeakably precious things: freedom of speech, freedom of conscience, and the prudence never to practice either of them.

PETER: What about our heritage?

TWAIN: The world and the books are so accustomed to use, and overuse, the word "new" in connection with our country, that we early get and permanently retain the impression that there is nothing old about it.

PETER: Do you admire our early leaders?

TWAIN: George Washington, as a boy, was ignorant of the commonest accomplishments of youth. He could not even lie. I am different from Washington; I have a higher, grander standard of principle. Washington could not lie. I can lie, but I won't.

PETER: If you won't be serious about the past, what about the present liberal-conservative struggle in this country?

TWAIN: The radical of one century is the conservative of the next. The radical invents the views. When he has worn them out the conservative adopts them.

PETER: What changes do you recommend?

TWAIN: Nothing so needs reforming as other people's habits.

PETER: Should more people speak out on the issues?

TWAIN: It's better to keep your mouth shut and appear stupid than to open it and remove all doubt.

PETER: You often give the impression that you are surrounded by fools.

TWAIN: Let us be thankful for the fools. But for them the rest of us could not succeed.

PETER: Will you tell me the secret of your success?

TWAIN: Part of the secret of success in life is to eat what you like and let the food fight it out inside.

PETER: You have been an adventurer and world traveler, but you have avoided trouble most of the time.

TWAIN: There are several good protections against temptation, but the surest is cowardice.

PETER: How about the troubles you have had?

TWAIN: I am an old man and have known a great many
troubles, but most of them never happened.

SECRETS OF SUCCESS

Recently I accepted an invitation to speak at a conference
of the Southern California Chapter, American Society of
Journalists and Authors. The topic assigned was "From Idea
to Best Seller." The more I thought about the subject, the
more aware I became that I had no formula for success to
present to my audience. I realized that no author ever intended to write anything but national best sellers, so I concluded that a national best seller is written in the same way as
a flop.

In spite of my lack of formulas for success, I did my best

to provide my listeners with—if not grand revelations—at least some helpful hints. During the question period the participants asked many questions about the actual process of writing. As I was being bombarded by questions, it occurred to me that interest in successful writers was intense. So, although the act of writing is usually a private affair, I am going to share with you some of the usually secret behavior of successful contemporary writers.

Most authors do their best work in seclusion and go to great lengths to assure their privacy. Harold Robbins has provided his rooftop studio in Le Cannet, France, with an electric ladder as the only means of access. Upon entering his studio, he flips a switch that retracts and locks the ladder out of reach of possible invaders. He walled up the picture window, with its grand view of the Mediterranean, because he found it distracting.

Ray Bradbury pedals his bicycle to his office, which, by the way, has no telephone.

When William Faulkner was employed as a writer for Warner Brothers Pictures, he lived in an apartment in Hollywood and worked at the studio. One day he approached the head of the story department and explained that he would prefer to write at home. Weeks later, when they tried to locate him, they found that he had returned to his permanent home in Oxford, Mississippi.

There is as much variety in the actual performance of the writing task as there is in the settings in which it occurs. While Gwen Bristow writes daily from 9:30 A.M to 12:30 P.M. and revises during the afternoon, Harrison Brown spends all day finding excuses for not writing and gets around to the actual task only by nightfall. He claims that the most time-consuming element in writing is getting started.

Mel Brooks has more difficulty finishing writing a movie script than he does in getting started, so he traps himself into completing the script. He does that by writing three pages and giving it to a movie company. If the movie makers like it, he makes a step deal—that is, they agree to pay so much for a rough treatment, so much for a first draft, then so much for a finished screenplay. Elliott Arnold also uses a system to keep him going. He stops each day's writing in mid-sentence.

Jack Douglas, using two fingers on a 1930 Remington typewriter, writes at a desk consisting of a sheet of plywood supported by two wooden horses. His reference system consists of a bulletin board loaded with notes, clippings, and written scraps of information. Steve Allen uses a dictating machine for nonfiction, a typewriter for fiction, and longhand for poetry and lyrics. Joe McGinnis simultaneously resigned his newspaper job, stopped drinking and smoking, and started exercising when he became a book writer. Rex Reed eats raw sweet potatoes while writing. Irving Wallace does his writing on a typewriter his parents gave him for his thirteenth birthday.

Well, that's a sample of what writers do behind closed doors. Unfortunately, for those interested in authors' idiosyncrasies, I must confess that my approach to writing is businesslike, logical, efficient, and well organized. My office is next to my bedroom, thus reducing travel time to a minimum. This convenient arrangement also eliminates the time and effort many authors waste on getting dressed. As writing requires no special uniform, I solve the problem by wearing none.

I write with a long quill. Not one of those old-fashioned quill pens, but a modern ball-point pen with a large pheasant feather attached. This has resolved my former problem of frequently misplacing my pen. No matter how many papers are piled on my desk, at least the tip of the feather is poking out somewhere.

Before I became so efficient, I used to worry as I approached the bottom of a page that I wouldn't get all of the last sentence on that sheet of paper. I resolved the problem by writing on one long roll of paper attached to an empty juice can. These scrolls, one per chapter, are rolled up or unrolled as required without the danger of loss or confusion created by the separate-sheet system.

I am sure that you can readily see it is in the interest of efficiency that I sit here in the nude, writing with my quill pen on this scroll. I think it can be fairly said that although there is great variation in writers' habits, there are generally two types of writers: those, like me, who are organized and businesslike about their craft and those with strange behaviors.

KING OF THE ONE-LINERS

Recently I have heard Elbert Hubbard being quoted with increasing frequency by persons of the right, center, and left. Usually, when I inquired about who was being quoted, either my questions drew a blank or my informant said it was a quote by newspaper columnist Kin Hubbard. So the following is presented as a public service.

Elbert Hubbard was born in Bloomington, Illinois, on June 19, 1856. Dropping out of high school, he entered the business world, where he became a pioneer in the field of employee relations and advertising. Later he gave up a successful business career to become a prolific writer and one of the highest-paid lecturers in America.

He was not concerned with fashions in appearance or thought. His long hair and flowing, soft black tie were not the style of his day, and his writings were a strange mixture of conservatism and radicalism. He knew the importance of communicating a point in as few words as possible. Even his longest discourses consisted of a well-connected series of epigrams.

Hubbard met his death on May 7, 1915, as a passenger of the ill-fated *Lusitania,* so all his answers to my contemporary questions are from his published works.[4]

PETER: I appreciate your granting me this interview.

HUBBARD: Nothing is so pleasant as to air our worldly wisdom in epigrammatic nuggets. To sit quiet and listen to another do it—well, that is another matter!

PETER: Does your controversial mixture of liberal and conservative messages bring you much criticism?

HUBBARD: Just why all the cranks in the United States should write me letters, I do not know: but they do. Perhaps there is a sort o' fellow feeling.

PETER: Many write to you for advice. What is your most frequent recommendation?

HUBBARD: Just you please listen to my advice: take nobody's.

PETER: To what do you attribute your success?

HUBBARD: To loom up large in life, get close to the camera.

PETER: Why do you profess belief in God, yet criticize religion?

HUBBARD: This religious farce is a hell of a plan. God looked upon His work and saw that it was good. That is where the clergy took issue with Him. Religions are many and diverse, but reason and goodness are one.

PETER: You are not very charitable toward the clergy.

HUBBARD: An ounce of performance is worth more than a pound of preachment. Two-thirds of all preachers, doctors and lawyers are hanging on to the coattails of progress, shouting whoa! while a good many of the rest are busy strewing banana peels along the line of march.

PETER: But don't your beliefs constitute a kind of religion?

HUBBARD: I recommend a religion that will unite men, not divide them. The only sin is to be unkind. Love is the one Divine thing in the Universe. God has it in His special keeping. There is only one thing worth praying for: to be in the line of evolution.

PETER: My readers would appreciate an explanation of another anomaly. You are intensely patriotic, yet you continue to be critical of the military.

HUBBARD: The soldier and the priest have wrecked every land where they have had the power. And the worst part about making a soldier of a man is not that a soldier kills brown men or white men, but that the soldier loses his own soul. The ink of the wise is of more value than the blood of the martyrs.

PETER: This brings me to the question of education's contribution to a better world.

HUBBARD: A school should not be a preparation for life. A school should be life.

PETER: Can education resolve our national dilemmas?

HUBBARD: This will never be a civilized country until we spend more money for books than we do for chewing-gum.

PETER: What then do you consider to be the major aim of education?

HUBBARD: The object of teaching a child is to enable him to get along without his teacher.

PETER: Are the teachers doing a good job?

HUBBARD: I hear that New York schoolteachers tell the children that the Devil is loose on Manhattan Isle; and the worst of it is, it's true.

PETER: And how about college?

HUBBARD: A college degree is a social certificate, not a proof of competence. You can lead a boy to college, but you cannot make him think. A college degree does not lessen the length of your ears; it only conceals it.

PETER: What is your concept of personal success?

HUBBARD: Success is the realization of the estimate which you place upon yourself.

PETER: And your formula for achieving it?

HUBBARD: Be pleasant until ten o'clock in the morning and the rest of the day will take care of itself.

PETER: You have said that your most creative work is in your philosophical epigrams.

HUBBARD: The delight of creative work lies in self-discovery —you are mining nuggets of power out of your own cosmos, and the find comes as a great and glad surprise.

PETER: Have you been able to define genius?

HUBBARD: Genius is the ability to act wisely without precedent—the power to do the right thing for the first time.

PETER: You disapprove of our throwaway society.

HUBBARD: Power manifests itself in conspicuous waste, and the habit grows until conspicuous waste imagines itself power.

PETER: What is your personal attitude toward possessions?

HUBBARD: I would rather be able to appreciate things I cannot have than to have things I am not able to appreciate. Too many people nowadays know the price of everything and the value of nothing.

PETER: But doesn't value depend to a large extent on personal performance?

HUBBARD: All that glitters is not brass.

PETER: That answer is one of your many humorous epigrams. What are some of your favorites?

HUBBARD: A conservative is a man who is too cowardly to fight and too fat to run.

All things come too late for those who wait.

While five o'clock tea may not work, eleven o'clock beer is a roaring success.

Two in the bush is the root of all evil.

PETER: Now how about some of your epigrams that express your philosophy of life?

HUBBARD: It is a curious fact that of all the illusions that beset mankind none is quite so curious as that tendency to suppose that we are mentally and morally superior to those who differ from us in opinion.

Truth is that which serves us best in expressing our lives.

A rotting log is truth to a bed of violets; while sand is truth to a cactus.

If we are ever damned it will not be because we have loved too much, but because we have loved too little.

Do not take life too seriously—you will never get out of it alive.

CHAPTER 2

More Psycho Than Logical

WOULD YOU LIKE TO GAIN INSIGHT INTO THE HUMAN MIND that you never had before and much less imagined? This chapter may be just what you are looking for. If you accept anything that follows as being scientifically accurate, you should have your head examined.

There are never enough certified therapists, psychologists, psychiatrists, and counselors to go around. Obviously many more therapists are needed to deal with the proliferating emotional difficulties generated by environmental deterioration, pollution, computers, the sexual revolution, inflation, punk rock, and other distressing conditions. We are living in stressful times—at least I am.

I have been a psychologist for most of my adult life and recently have noticed that many of my colleagues, and other social scientists specializing in treating the hapless, are dividing their thoughts and feelings into logic-tight compartments. This makes it extremely difficult for the layperson to know what is going on. On the other hand, there is a handful of well-meaning practitioners writing popular articles and appearing on radio and television offering advice. These psychologists are unremitting in their campaign to explain psychology to the people and simplify the arguments that exist within the profession. My purpose in writing this chapter is to stem this dangerous trend and help maintain the time-honored tradition of the profession by creating as much confusion as possible.

MAIER'S LAW

Modern psychology is divided by differences in theoretical position or philosophical thought. Unfortunately, in spite of great promises, no one school of psychology has yet produced an effective remedy for the pathology of the human condition. Mankind is still beset by neurosis, psychosis, violence, and other self-destructive or maladaptive behavior.

You may find the following psychological laws to be helpful, whatever your psychological beliefs. Even if you don't learn much psychology, a little laughter relieves the dullness to which the study of psychology is prone. Maier's Law is presented first because of the universality of its application.

MAIER'S LAW: If facts do not conform to the theory, they must be disposed of.

—N. R. F. MAIER

Maier first presented his law in the March 1960 issue of *The American Psychologist* as an explanation to other psychologists to show them how they can obtain positive research results through the process of ignoring negative data. For example, in conducting an experiment in which laboratory rats are required to learn the intricacies of maze running, it is discovered that twelve of the rats do not learn the task that is crucial to the theory being tested. The application of Maier's Law requires that the twelve uncooperative rats be dropped from the experiment. In carefully conducted experiments, it is not necessary to destroy the uncooperative subjects. If the experiment is arranged successfully, the undesirable rats will fail to negotiate the maze to obtain the reward of food and will expire from starvation or, in cases of extreme necessity, neglect.

In working with human subjects, such as in a classroom learning experiment, starvation of the uncooperative or slow-learning children is not necessary if the researcher assures that these experimentally undesirable pupils fail the tests and are transferred to special classes.

The beauty of Maier's Law is that it applies to many fields of human endeavor, not only psychology. It can be applied by anyone who understands that when the facts do not support the theory, one must change the facts. A useful extension of Maier's Law is provided by Spinoza.

SPINOZA'S LAW: If facts conflict with a theory, either the theory must be changed or the facts.

—BENEDICT SPINOZA

LEVENSON'S LAW: Insanity is hereditary; you can get it from your children.

—SAM LEVENSON

The Buxton *Advertiser* carried the following announcement: "On Wednesday there will be a meeting for all new pupils and their parents. This is to give them an opportunity to get to know each other." Although there may be no serious danger in this, parents can suffer disturbances of their thought processes if they listen too closely to their children. Parents are particularly vulnerable when asked, "Know what I learned in school today?" In response to "No, what did you learn in school today?" parents have been supplied with gems, such as:

How to puncture a paragraph.
The first person to go to the moon was a monkey.
They have the Fourth of July all over the world.
All the kids in my class have been intoxicated for smallpox.
Carl Sandburg got a Pullet Surprise for his poems.
The main use of petroleum is to make some people rich.

Charles van Kriedt reported a group discussion about a politician in which one participant observed, "I don't think they could put him in a mental hospital. On the other hand, if he were already in, I don't believe they'd let him out."

KRIEDT'S LAW: Sanity and insanity overlap a fine gray line.

SELECTING A SCHOOL COUNSELOR

Statement of the Problem

The purpose of this study was to establish standards for school counselor selection based upon the personal characteristics that contribute to counselor success.*

* This problem was treated more fully in Justin Case, "Counseling, Its Cause and Cure," *PAP* (*Philosophic Aspects of Pedagogy*) (June 1960).

Type A—Desirable

Design of the Study

Research has investigated behavior changes in laboratory rats but has made a limited contribution to the understanding of counseling. The rat has not been a cooperative subject for studies of counseling or psychotherapy.* Furthermore, it was recognized that the counselor was in a profession where, by definition, the customer was always wrong. This kind of value judgment was not appropriate in rat experiments.

Guidance methods have established vocational placement on the basis of relating personal characteristics to occupational requirements. This technique has been overlooked in the selection of the counselors themselves. Therefore, the research

---

* A. Mammal, in his monumental work *Psychoanalysis of the Rat: Its Implication Up and Down the Phylogenetic Scale*, reported that his client gnawed a hole in his couch.

Type V—Undesirable

design for the present study was based upon this matching process. A time-and-motion study was undertaken, and the job description outlined.

Summary of Findings

The findings were summarized in terms of job requirements as related to physical characteristics, general and emotional health, and personality development.*

PHYSICAL CHARACTERISTICS. The motion study showed that counselors spent long periods of time seated behind a desk,

* This is a progress report and does not include all characteristics studied. As funds and staff become available, further reports will be released.

remaining comparatively still. It was observed that certain physical characteristics were significant in determining success in this activity. Body types were studied, and correlations established.* It was reliably determined that sitting success was dependent upon a low center of gravity. Two body types were defined. The unsuitable classification, Sedentary-Physique-Type V Negative, consisted of big-bosomed females and broad-shouldered, narrow-hipped males who were top-heavy and under constant strain to maintain balance. The suitable classification, Sedentary-Physique-Type A Positive, consisted of those with broad hips that provided a solid base upon which the body was easily balanced. They had narrow, sloping shoulders and well-developed chests resting just below the waistline. The head was rather small and pointed,† completing the A shape and presenting a pleasingly regular picture of stability in the sitting position. Although the legs were not actively involved, it was observed that short legs, barely reaching the floor, kept the counselor on his toes.

GENERAL HEALTH.   Counselors were observed for any significant health problem relating to their effectiveness. A case study will show how the Counselor-Health-Therapy Principle was discovered. Counselor X had an enviable reputation as a nondirective therapist.‡ When he responded with a nod of his head and vocal utterance (*hrmpff*), his client, satisfied with this behavior, resumed his discourse about himself. Later it was noticed that the couselor continued the head movement between interviews. When it was revealed that Counselor X had an affliction that caused these involuntary movements, it

---

* Similar studies relating to body types have been reported by Lombroso, Galton, Kretschmer, and Sheldon.

† X. Y. Zee, M.A., M.Sc., D.D., "Headgear Sizing: A Correlation with Counseling Ability," *QED (Quotable Educational Documents)* (October 1960).

‡ A form of supportive therapy in which the counselor assumes a neutral role and responds to the clients' statements with sounds or gestures of ambiguous meaning.

was concluded that success was the result of a nervous tic. As the research progressed, it became apparent that any observable unhealthy condition in the counselor had therapeutic effect for the client. A few examples will serve to illustrate the universality of this principle.*

Counselor Y was asthmatic. It was obvious that clients became aware of his difficult breathing. It would be beneficial if no more were accomplished than getting clients' concern away from their own troubles, but the transference of attention from their own difficulties to those of the counselor was only a first step in therapy. Some clients became so concerned regarding the counselor's health that they declined to mention personal difficulties.

Counselor Z, suffering from severe health problems, was in considerable pain. It was interesting to observe clients, during successive interviews, becoming hardened to suffering and therefore developing a capacity for dealing more effectively with problems. Furthermore, the clients with psychosomatic, emotional, or imaginary illnesses, upon seeing the real distress of Counselor Z, were willing to give up their symptoms, feeling they were comparatively well.

It was concluded that almost any illness contributed to counselor effectiveness.

EMOTIONAL HEALTH. All counselors in this study had been classroom teachers and claimed they had left their instructional assignment voluntarily. While some admitted to being malcontents in the classroom situation, others expressed the need to have a unique occupation within the profession. Sufficiently dissatisfied with being teachers, being like other teachers, or being called regular classroom teachers, they gave up their

* Some books soon to be released may shed new light on the positive value of certain deviations: Spike D. Hood, *Delinquency for Fun and Profit*, Juvenile Books, Inc.; Mort Titian, *The Death Wish*, Embalmer's Publishing and Packing Co.; Betty Gains, *Eat and Grow Fat*, Healthways Publishers; Al K. Hall, *How to Increase Your Drinking Power*, WCTU Press, Inc.

lifework to become counselors. Unless they were maladjusted and needed to be different from normal teachers, it was improbable that real success and contentment would be found in counseling.

Counselors were required to deal with the sordid aspects of life and to work at greater depth with problems of delinquency, family disintegration, failure, cheating, and so forth. Unless the counselor showed more than normal interest in deviations, little was found to sustain enthusiasm. Emotionally, therefore, the counselor was described as a teacher who had become a malcontent, who was maladjusted, and who had a preoccupation with morbidity.

PERSONALITY DEVELOPMENT. Unlike regular classroom teachers, counselors in this study worked exclusively with clients of their own sex. This preference made special personality demands for which a homosexual personality component seemed appropriate. Because homosexuality is a relative matter, it was not recommended that individuals be ideally suited, in any absolute sense, to be acceptable for counseling positions.

It was observed that clients came to counselors to unburden themselves of hostilities, anxieties, and a variety of troubles. The successful counselor was able to absorb hostility and take on an extra burden of suffering. To derive satisfaction from seeking more pain than normally experienced required the counselor to be somewhat masochistic.*

* *Sadism in School Administration: The Cane, Birch Rod, and Strap as Related to the Pleasure-Pain Syndrome.* The author, I. M. Profound, states: "Teachers move from the classroom in two directions. The masochist moves toward counseling. The sadist moves toward administration. The opportunities in administration for infliction of suffering appear unlimited when one considers timetable construction, establishment of failure rates, supervision schedules, school rules, teacher reports, and punishment of children. The counselor and administrator are at opposite ends of a continuum. This brings into question the logic of the common practice of selecting administrators from the ranks of counselors."

Conclusion

The individual who possessed this combination of character-istics was ideally suited for the school counselor role.

The fact that a statement of these standards had not ap-peared before was a tribute to counselors' dedication to their duties. This study revealed that they had been so busy match-ing clients' characteristics with the requirements of various vocational and educational placements that they had neither time nor energy left with which to apply these techniques to their own profession.

In conclusion, it should be stated that these are not new standards. A process of natural selection has been going on ever since school counseling began, and certain individuals have found in counseling that niche which suited them best. This, however, should not be an excuse for complacency. If the principle of natural selection is valid, then these standards are in reality the old standards newly described.

By employing the criteria implied herein, much of the trial-and-error method of counselor selection can be eliminated, and greater efficiency in the deployment of teaching staff can be achieved. Administrators can now be assured that only suitable candidates be accepted for this key position in the education of our children.

THE TWELVE-WORD CURE

Back in the early twenties, when I was a small boy living in Vancouver, B.C., Canada, I observed adults muttering or chanting as they walked along the street or rode in the trolley cars. When I asked my mother about what seemed to me strange behavior, she told me they were practicing Couéism. As quickly as this craze for talking to oneself had started, it disappeared, and people once more spoke to those they met as they passed along the wooden sidewalks of our sparsely

populated suburb or shared a wicker seat in a B.C. Electric
Railway Company streetcar. Although I didn't know it at the
time, I had been witness to the most popular psychotherapy
fad of all time.

The widespread acceptance of Couéism by the general public was probably due to the simplicity of its method of treatment which consisted of frequent repetitions of the formula
"Every day, and in every way, I am becoming better and better." No examinations, no pills, no textbooks, no therapist ses-
sions, just a simple self-help technique that held great promise.

The founder of this school of "psychology," as it was called,
was Émile Coué. He was born on February 26, 1857, in
Troyes, France, and became a pharmacist in his hometown
in 1882. While continung to practice his profession, he began
the study of hypnotism under Liébault and Bernheim at Nancy
in 1901. In 1920, at his own clinic, he introduced a system
of healing called Self-Mastery by Autosuggestion. His success
in France was followed by appearances in London, where

his lectures and demonstrations attracted large audiences and brought forth endorsements from members of the nobility, including such highly regarded individuals as Earl Curzon and Lady Beatty.

It is little wonder that his arrival on United States shores in 1923, with his promise of the blessings of health and happiness, was the answer to a publicity man's prayers. After a hectic Atlantic crossing through a succession of storms the ship arrived at its Manhattan dock. Most of the passengers were pale and weak from long periods of seasickness. Émile Coué, the small, rotund Frenchman with gray hair and neat Vandyke beard, bounded ashore and announced to the assembled news reporters that he had had a most pleasurable voyage.

Headlines proclaimed that the "Pied Piper of Contentment" had arrived. This image, bolstered by well-planned advance notices, attracted large crowds for his lectures on his triumphal cross-country tour, which called for his return visit in 1924.

Coué proclaimed that his prescription could cure many ailments and even grow hair on bald heads. A number of individuals came forth to endorse Couéism and give testimony about their cures, but nobody claimed to be cured of baldness. Many of Coué's followers called him a miracle worker, but he made no such claim. He said, "I am not a miracle man. I do not heal people. I teach them to cure themselves."

The influence of Couéism grew rapidly. A magazine devoted to Couéism contained many case histories of cures attributed to the twelve-word Rx. Coué institutes were established in cities across the country. The famous Shakespearean actor E. H. Sothern endorsed Couéism. Dr. Henry Fairfield Osborn, president of the American Museum of Natural History, stated, "American high-speed life needs the calming effects of Couéism." Although the American Medical Association condemned his methods and denounced him as a "purveyor of cloudy stuff," Dr. George Draper of New York's Presbyterian Hospital said that M. Coué had stripped disease of its dignity by getting people to believe in their own regenerative powers. Pastors preached about the virtues of Couéism, and even the usually restrained Daughters of the American Revolution invited him to come to Washington to speak and to demonstrate his cures.

As Coué's influence escalated so did his claims of success. He had received some opposition for his statement that auto-suggestion could cure baldness, but now he was claiming that it could dictate, in advance of birth, the sex of a baby. If an expectant mother wanted a baby girl, all she had to do was say over and over again each day, "My child will be a girl." He also claimed that a mother could predetermine her off-spring's career by practicing autosuggestive thoughts during her pregnancy. "If she wants her unborn son to be a great architect she should visit great buildings and surround herself with pictures of architectural masterpieces and above all she should think beautiful thoughts." He went on to claim that Couéism could solve social problems and that autosuggestion, by digging the bad ideas out of the subconscious mind, could reduce delinquency, crime, and vice. The scientific community was quick to attack with claims that M. Coué didn't know what he was talking about.

Although Coué lacked the support of authorities with spe-cial skill and knowledge, his influence was great. Not only did the people in the big cities where he lectured become followers, but the inhabitants of the small towns and rural areas of England, Canada, and the United States who knew of the twelve-word cure only through reading about it in the newspapers, began chanting, "Every day, and in every way. . . ."

The 1924 tour failed to repeat the 1923 triumph. Coué's message of optimism was a short-lived fad that captured the public imagination for a season and then faded rapidly. Not content with his earlier success in treating minor functional disorders, he escalated himself to his level of incompetence by promising much more than he could possibly deliver. He proclaimed "better and better"; but many of his followers did not improve, and some got worse and worse.

He returned to France and his clinic at Nancy, but his practice declined as clients failed to show up. On July 2, 1926, M. Coué died of a heart attack. Because I had not heard the name Coué mentioned in many years, I was convinced that Couéism had been forgotten. But then I read a recent article in the *New York Times Magazine* about the treatment of pain. It described how Dr. C. Norman Shealy's Pain and Health Rehabilitation Center in La Crosse, Wisconsin, has patients sitting in reclining chairs reciting (among other things) M. Coué's "Every day, and in every. . . ." Contemplating this resurrection of an old concept, I revised the Peter Principle to read: "When an idea rises to its level of incompetence, it may die, be buried for fifty years, and still rise again."

SLUMBERING INSPIRATION

Over the years my accomplishments have been the result of painstaking attention to detail. I had often wished there were a less time-consuming method. Therefore, I was particularly interested in an article by William B. Werther, Jr., in which he stated, "Many authors have awakened in the middle of the night and outlined successful novels or penned poems or musical scores." He went on to explain that frequently the subconscious continues to work on problems during sleep, and upon one's waking a clue or even the entire solution pops into the conscious mind. Could this be the answer to my dilemma? Had I been trying too hard and overworking my conscious mind? Should I turn over the idea department to my subconscious and see what it could come up with? Two things were obvious: I had been doing things the hard way, and my subconscious must have been goofing off because I wasn't conscious of my subconscious doing much.

Two points in Werther's article seemed of particular im-

portance: "Although much is written about the subconscious, very little is known about it," and "Scientists are reasonably convinced, however, that illuminations occur when the mind is relaxed." What a relief to find a formula that was so simple with results so promising.

> *WERTHER'S LAW: Relax your mind, and let your sub- conscious be your guide.*

I knew the validity of this spontaneous-subconscious-in-spiration process because many times I had been awakened in the night by a brilliant idea passing through my mind. Un-fortunately by morning I was only vaguely aware of the details of the revelation of the night before. Try as I would through-out my waking hours, the vision that was crystal-clear during the night would return only as an incomplete, blurred image. The solution recommended by Werther was so obvious that I resented the fact I had not thought of it earlier. One must write down the inspiration immediately, before sleep returns to rob the mind of the clarity of the vision.

I systematically prepared for the night's work by placing a flashlight, pen, and paper on the bedside table. I wish to report that the preparation worked perfectly. I awoke with the secret of success revealed to me. I wrote it down rapidly and drifted back to sleep. The next morning I read, "Collect performance royalties." It was probaby a good idea, but to this day I have been unable to figure out for what performances I should try to collect royalties. A few mornings later a more fitting message appeared on my notepaper: "Sufficient unto the day is the drivel thereof."

Not being too thrilled with my own subconscious, I turned my attention to the night writing of famous men of letters. William James had a dream in which the secret of life was revealed. He hastily scribbled it down, and the next morning read:

Higamus, Hogamus, Women are Monogamous,
Hogamus, Higamus, Men are Polygamous.

Ralph Waldo Emerson was a devotee of night writing, so he kept a pad, pencil, and matches near his bed. The wooden matches used in his time came in a strip. One night he awoke to write down an eloquent concept. He broke off a match, but it wouldn't light. He broke off another, but it was also a dud. He kept trying until all the matches were broken off. The next morning he was still annoyed by his failure to obtain a light and was even more disturbed when his wife asked him, "What has happened to my tortoiseshell comb? All the teeth are broken off."

I was about ready to give up on the Werther method when I read about Sir Frederick G. Banting's discovery of the isolation of insulin and thereby the control of diabetes. At 2:00 A.M., October 30, 1920, he leaped out of bed and scribbled fourteen words describing a medical breakthrough: "Tie off pancreas ducts of dogs. Wait six or eight weeks. Remove and extract."

THE MEACHAM MEASUREMENT

While reading the Jimmy Carter interview in *Playboy*, I was particularly interested in his confession that he had "lusted in his heart" for several women. I wasn't fascinated by Carter's sex life; it was simply that the thought of Carter's coveting a number of women reminded me of an experience I had early in my graduate studies. One of my professors, Dr. Merle L. Meacham, the eminent behavioral psychologist, asked a number of male students to help collect some data for his research project. Those who volunteered were divided into teams according to age and given their assignments. We were to count and keep a record of the number of females observed and the number coveted. We were also encouraged to calculate our own coveting rates (CR). For example, as I walked across the campus one sunny day in spring, I took careful notice of twelve females. I coveted (lusted in my heart for) three. Therefore, my coveting rate for this particular sample was 25 percent.

In the intervening years I had often considered inquiring of my old professor what he did with our data, but it took the Carter confession to stimulate me into action. I made an appointment and visited Dr. Meacham in his office at the University of Washington.

The years had been kind to the aging professor. He had gained a few pounds, and his formerly dark hair was now a mane of wavy silvery gray, but otherwise he seemed unchanged.

After the usual exchange of pleasantries I asked him to describe the purpose of his research. He leaned back in his chair and offered this explanation.

An alarming number of middle-age males suffer from a condition variously called the male menopause, mid-life panic, loss of identity, male climacteric, or identity crisis. The purpose of the research was to discover if this male crisis could be predicted and maybe even averted.

What the research revealed was that as a male person grows older, his coveting rate increases while his consummation rate decreases. In other words, up until the male climacteric, the point at which the Meacham Droop sets in, sexual desire outstrips sexual satisfaction.

At this point in our discussion Dr. Meacham pointed to a large diagram hanging by a string so that it could be turned to face the wall. After examining it, I made this hasty sketch.

Carefully lettered beneath the diagram was the following definition:

THE MEACHAM MEASUREMENT: A scale of sexual frustration represented by the difference between the male coveting response and the consummation rate.

After I finished examining the diagram, Dr. Meacham went on with his explanation. He described the illustration as a visual representation of the pattern of sexual coveting and consummation of the average male and pointed out that

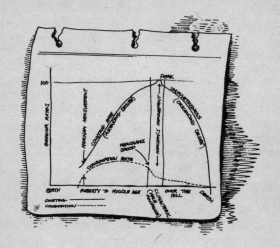

although there were wide individual differences in the responses of the subjects in his study, the overall pattern remained constant throughout.

Whether for cultural or biological reasons it seemed that males tended to desire all females their own age and younger down to the age when coveting began, roughly puberty. So the coveting rate was cumulative and steadily increased as the subject approached middle age.

At that point in life, when the Meacham Measurement reaches its peak, the individual becomes aware that his sexual prowess may be on the wane. Panic takes over, and he suffers a brief spell of impotence, seen in the illustration as the Meacham Droop. The thought that he is over the hill results in depression, a flurry of sexual activity, confusion, thoughts of impending death, identity problems, and other symptoms associated with the male menopause or climacteric.

Dr. Meacham's present exploration is focused on attempts

to find a viable therapeutic solution. The obvious answer, he claimed, is to reduce the Meacham Measurement to within acceptable limits, but he is unable to decide whether it will be more feasible to lower the subject's coveting rate or to increase his consummation rate.

When I suggested that his study was the most sexist piece of research I had ever seen, he wholeheartedly agreed and claimed that physical factors made it imperative that male and female studies be conducted separately. In defense of his argument he quoted Mark Twain: "The candle holder will far outlast the candle." And then to my astonishment he proposed that we collaborate on a study to verify that biologically the female is ideally equipped to satisfy her coveting responses. I panicked and stammered my apologies as I dashed from the office in utter confusion.

FREUD'S GREAT DISCOVERY

When Sigmund Freud (1856–1939) embarked upon his study of the mind, psychology was still a branch of philosophy. His predecessors had presumed that because the mind was invisible and intangible, the only way of delving into its function was through introspection. In other words, mental research consisted of the investigator's mind studying itself. Then, in a three-year period from 1892 to 1895, Freud, a medical doctor specializing in nervous diseases, developed a therapeutic modality he called psychoanalysis.

In Freudian analysis the patient lies on a couch and free-associates or talks about anything that comes into his or her mind. Originally Freud estimated that psychoanalysis would be a relatively short treatment, but with experience he recommended that the patients see the analyst three to five times a week for several years and in some cases for the rest of the patient's life.

Although Freudian psychoanalysis is still practiced in its pure form by some of his followers, many psychotherapists felt that it was too time-consuming and attempted to shorten the process. This impatience is partly responsible for the ever-growing number of variations on Freud's original theme as well as for many new therapies. Although I cannot but admire the zeal of these innovators and critics of Freud, it is my purpose, here, to expose the fallacy of their methods.

The first real evidence regarding the effectiveness of psychotherapy was provided by Hans J. Eysenck in 1952.[5] In his now historic monograph he reported on two groups of adults who had neurotic disorders—a group of 7,293 that received psychotherapy and a control group that received no therapy or medication. He concluded that roughly two-thirds of the neurotics recover within two years of the onset of their illness, whether they receive psychotherapy or not.

Time shall teach thee all things.
—GEORGE SHARSWOOD (1810–1883)

Levitt (1957)[6] reported on the results of psychotherapy with 7,987 children as compared with an untreated control group. There was no significant difference in the outcomes for the two groups. He concluded that time was the important factor in the children's recovery from emotional disturbance.

Time hath a taming hand.
    —JOHN CARDINAL NEWMAN (1801–1890)

The Cambridge-Somerville Study (McCord and McCord, 1959)[7] investigated the effect of preventive psychotherapy on potential delinquents. Six hundred and fifty underprivileged, behavior-disordered boys were divided into two equal groups. The treated boys received therapy from counselors using Freudian and Rogerian methods. The experiment lasted eight years, after which time the boys in each group were evaluated. The untreated boys proved to have fewer delinquent episodes than the treated group, but over time there was not a significant difference in the rate of delinquency in the two groups.

For time will teach thee soon the truth.
    —HENRY WADSWORTH LONGFELLOW
    (1807–1882)

This research makes it abundantly clear that *time* is the effective ingredient in the reduction or cure of neurotic symptoms. It demonstrates that psychotherapy is as effective as whatever else people do who are not in therapy. It was the genius of Sigmund Freud that produced a comprehensive, systematic model for the application of the *therapeutic-time concept*. Unfortunately the real significance of protracted psychoanalysis is not at all clearly understood by many psychotherapists, psychiatrists, and psychologists. They fail to heed the age-old advice "Time heals all wounds" and are more in tune with Jane Ace's "Time wounds all heels."

Healing is a matter of time, but it is sometimes a matter of opportunity.

—HIPPOCRATES (c. 460–337 B.C.)

Time as he grows old teaches many lessons.

—AESCHYLUS (525–456 B.C.)

Time will explain it all.

—EURIPIDES (c. 484–c. 406 B.C.)

Be ruled by time, the wisest counselor of all.

—PLUTARCH (A.D. c. 46–c. 120)

Time, that aged nurse,
Rock'd me to patience.

—JOHN KEATS (1795–1821)

Time is the only comforter. . . .

—JANE WELSH CARLYLE (1801–1866)

Remember that time is money.

—BENJAMIN FRANKLIN (1706–1790)

CHAPTER 3

Let Me Entertain You

EACH OF THE PERSONS WE SHALL VISIT IN THIS CHAPTER HAS contributed something unique to help fulfill our need to be entertained.

P. T. Barnum is credited with creating the Greatest Show on Earth, but his most important accomplishment was one that is seldom written about. He influenced American history in far more profound ways than did many of our famous political and military heroes written about in history books.

James McNeill Whistler, the great American artist, is not usually considered an entertainer, and certainly his accomplishments as a painter far outweigh whatever amusement we may garner from his eccentric behavior.

Joseph Pujol, a French vaudevillian, performed from 1892 to 1914 at the famous Moulin Rouge under the name of Le Petomane. His specialty was the public performance of an action that people in polite society try to suppress.

Will Rogers performed in Wild West shows, vaudeville, the *Ziegfeld Follies*, radio, and motion pictures but is probably best remembered for the wit of his remarks in his daily newspaper column and in his lectures. His ability to prick the bubble of pomposity wherever it appeared, without being offensive or partisan, was unique in the history of show business.

Johnny Carson is number one in a new entertainment role created by television, the talk-show host, and therefore deserves consideration in any discussion of show business today.

George Carlin has received national attention for using seven words in his act that led to charges of obscenity and court appearances. Of the many great comedians of today, Carlin is in the forefront of those who can be both consistently topical and funny.

AMERICA'S SHOWMAN

Will Rogers said, "We're all ignorant, but on different subjects." So don't feel too incompetent if you fail the following Dr. Peter competency test.

1. Did Washington throw a dollar across the Potomac?

2. Did Hamlet say, "Alas, poor Yorick: I knew him well"?
3. Did P. T. Barnum say, "There's a sucker born every minute"?

Answers:

1. No. He threw it across the Rappahannock.
2. No. He said, "Alas, poor Yorick! I knew him, Horatio: a fellow of infinite jest, of most excellent fancy."
3. No. The word "sucker," as a slang expression meaning one who is easily duped, did not come into our language until after Barnum's death. He did say, "The American people like to be humbugged," meaning that Americans could enjoy a joke even when it was on themselves. Usually, when Barnum admitted a hoax, his audience did not become hostile but laughed it off and came back for more. This characteristic of Americans was responsible for Barnum's success, and Barnum's success was responsible for shaping the character of America.

Although it is well known that Phineas Taylor Barnum [8] was the greatest showman of his time, or probably all time, it is not generally understood how great was his impact on American history. During the twenty years between 1835 and 1855, the time of Barnum's ascendancy in the world of show business, America changed from being a Victorian society of prudes to being a fun-loving nation of sport and entertainment enthusiasts. Barnum ushered in a new age—the age of showmanship.

In 1835, when Barnum was twenty-five, he read an advertisement in the newspaper that presented him with an opportunity to get out of the grocery business and get into show business. The ad offered for sale a Negress, Joice Heth, aged a hundred and sixty-one years, who had been a nurse for George Washington. Barnum rushed to Boston, where Joice Heth was on exhibit. After assuring himself that she was the genuine article, he purchased her and brought her to New York. The awesome appearance of this "living fossil," with her shrunken body and leathery, wrinkled skin, her fused joints and immobile frame, and her deeply sunken, blind eyes, was in contrast with her good spirits and phenomenal memory for the details of her servitude to the Washington family and of her duties in raising George.

Through newspaper advertising, displays of lavish posters, news releases about the discovery of the original bill of sale for Joice Heth, dated February 5, 1727, and other "scientific" evidence of her authenticity, Barnum was able to stimulate great public interest in his exhibit. When Joice Heth died a year later, an autopsy revealed she was about eighty years old. Barnum claimed that *he* had been the victim of a hoax.

Disclosure of the Joice Heth fraud did not dampen his enthusiasm for his career as an entrepreneur. Barnum, in an age when entertainment was thought to be the work of the devil, had aroused the curiosity of the public, had focused their attention on something outside their own struggles, had through a combination of fake scientific and pseudoeducational justification made the pursuit of fun legitimate. Barnum was more admired than resented, for America desperately needed the product he had to offer.

The American Museum, in New York, which he operated from 1842 to 1868, was his proudest accomplishment and attracted 82 million visitors to its exhibits of genuine and fake relics and curiosities.

Barnum promoted and displayed the Feejee Mermaid, which had been assembled from the head and upper torso of a monkey and the body and tail of a fish. He promoted and exhibited a twenty-five-inch midget, General Tom Thumb, in both America and Europe. Among his many successes were Chang and Eng, the original Siamese twins; the soprano Jenny Lind, billed as the Swedish Nightingale; Jumbo, the world's largest elephant; Josephine Clofullia, the bearded lady; James C. Adams, nicknamed Grizzly Adams, an old hunter and trapper who tamed and trained wild animals; and many more.

In mid-career he was world-famous, wealthy, and a little

bored with business, so he went into politics. In 1865 he was elected to the Connecticut legislature, where he worked to defeat the railway monopoly and supported the Thirteenth Amendment to abolish slavery. In 1875 he became mayor of Bridgeport, and in 1877 he was again elected to the Connecticut General Assembly.

Barnum, who had always considered himself an impresario and museum operator, became a circus owner only after he was past the age of sixty. He was not a circus pioneer as is popularly believed. Many small traveling circuses were in existence when he and James A. Bailey combined their circuses and presented "The Greatest Show on Earth." Like his other show business projects, the Barnum & Bailey Circus became the biggest and best.

Born on July 5, 1810, in Bethel, Connecticut, Barnum grew up under its oppressive Puritanism. Blue laws made riding in a carriage or on a horse illegal on Sundays. Swearing was punishable by flogging. Playing a game of cards could result in arrest. Entertainment was denounced as sinful. Stage shows or theater were forbidden by law.

Throughout his career Barnum crusaded to make life in America a sinless festival. Long before his death on April 7, 1891, his vision had become a reality. He had brought amusement and joy to a relatively cheerless world and made fun and laughter an acceptable part of the American way of life. He made several fortunes along the way and revealed the secret of his show business success in a statement that I have labeled:

BARNUM'S PRINCIPLE: Every crowd has a silver lining.
—P. T. BARNUM

THE GENTLE ART OF MAKING ENEMIES

Do you experience a letdown when you meet a famous

person and find that your mental image of the celebrity is shattered? I have a vivid recollection of my first and only personal encounter with the late great insult comic Jack E. Leonard. While I was waiting in the green room for my turn to appear on a television show, Mr. Leonard entered quietly and eased his great bulk into the chair next to mine. He introduced himself in a quiet and modest manner. During the conversation that ensued he drew me out about my work with handicapped children. I was impressed by what appeared to be a genuine warmth and intelligent concern for children with problems. When I inquired about his career, I had to ask specific questions in order to get him to talk. As a young man in Chicago he had worked as a lifeguard, weighing in at 360 pounds. At night he obtained occasional engagements as a comic. Continuing in his unpretentious manner, he explained that his set act was not well received, but that his insults aimed at hecklers were so successful that they became the basis of his style. The only funny line in our entire conversation was his explanation that he was a double-threat comedian. "I used to be billed as Fat Jack and did a lot of fat jokes, but I'm also bald, so when I lose weight, I do bald jokes."

Could this quiet man be the roaring colossus of pomposity that I had seen onstage hurling insults in all directions? Could this modest, almost shy man sitting next to me be the rude, outrageous, belligerent entertainer whose booming voice and combative manner had, on other occasions, convulsed his audience with laughter?

Once he was on camera I was reassured that here was the real Jack E. Leonard. When the host offered a friendly hand of greeting, Leonard bellowed, "Don't touch the star!" When the host spoke, Leonard looked bored and turned away, but soon returned in unrestrained aggravation with: "Why don't you put your teeth in backwards and bite your own throat?" During commercial breaks he returned to his quiet, self-effacing manner, but when the signal light came on, he responded with a stream of abuse. "You haven't an enemy in the world but all your friends hate you. . . . You're not yourself today—it's a big improvement. . . . You only open your mouth when you have nothing to say. . . . I just want to say—if you had lived, you would have been a very sick man."

The point in relating this incident is that we form our images of the famous from their public performances. We expect that the author of a particularly entertaining book will be a brilliant conversationalist and are dismayed when he or she turns out to be an egotistical bore. I retain enough innocence that I am still mildly astonished when I discover that an eminent philosopher's private life is chaotic, that a public figure radiating confidence is still in psychoanalysis after many years of treatment, and that the creator of a monumental architectural masterpiece is a petty little man. This contrast between a man and his work is the subject of the following Peter's People story.

WHISTLER'S PRINCIPLE: If other people are going to talk, conversation is simply impossible.
> —JAMES ABBOTT MCNEILL WHISTLER
> (1834–1903)

Whistler's most celebrated painting is a canvas he titled "Arrangement in Gray and Black, Number One." It is the portrait popularly known as "Whistler's Mother." A friend, admiring the portrait, jokingly remarked, "Who would have thought of you as having a mother?" Whistler retorted, "Yes indeed, and a very pretty bit of color she is."

Whistler was born in Massachusetts in 1834 but spent most of his sixty-nine years as an expatriate in France and England. His beautiful impressionistic nightscapes, portraits, and landscapes are in contrast with his vengeful behavior and waspish

remarks. When his collected correspondence was published in 1890, it was titled *The Gentle Art of Making Enemies.*

Throughout his illustrious career he was involved in many legal battles, including the winning of a suit against an art gallery for hanging one of his paintings upside down. When his excessive viciousness as a litigant became completely unwarranted, his solicitor suggested that his client try to be reasonable. Whistler replied, "When I pay you six-and-eightpence, I pay you six-and-eightpence for law, not justice."

On a balmy summer evening Whistler was walking with an acquaintance who commented on the clear skies and beautiful stars above. Whistler glanced heavenward and replied, "I would have done it differently."

He devoted himself to mastery of his painting technique to the point where the evidences of technique disappeared and the painting had the appearance of effortlessness. He described this viewpoint in these words: "To say of a picture, as is often said in its praise, that it shows great and earnest labor, is to say that it is incomplete and unfit for view."

He was particularly hostile toward critics and told one, "You should not say it is not good. You should say you do not like it; and then, you know, you're perfectly safe." One of his bon mots was: "I am not arguing with you, I'm telling you."

A lady asked him why he was so unpleasant. Whistler's reply was: "My dear, I will tell you a secret. Early in life I made the discovery that if one is delightful, one has to thrust the world away to keep from being bored to death." His reply to a question about the origin of genius was: "I can't tell you if genius is hereditary because heaven has granted me no off-spring."

Even his notorious friendship with Oscar Wilde eventually deteriorated as a result of his insulting references to Wilde's homosexuality. For instance, he suggested that a new Wilde drama be titled *The Bugger's Opera*. I wish I could report that Whistler's Principle paid off in terms of a lifetime of happiness and satisfaction, but unfortunately in his later years he lamented, "I'm lonesome; they are all dying; I have hardly a warm personal enemy left."

THE FULL-BLOWN TALENT OF LE PETOMANE

It has occurred to me that there may be many individuals who have unique aptitudes that could be developed into exploitable talents if they only realized the commercial possibilities of real specialization. The following true-life success story illustrates this important concept.

The subject of this brief biographical sketch is a Frenchman, Joseph Pujol (1857–1945), who achieved stardom in the theaters of Europe as Le Petomane.[9] In Paris at the height of his spectacular career he was paid more than the great Sarah Bernhardt. During her appearance at the Variety, the box-office receipts for one day were 8,000 francs, while at the Moulin Rouge, Le Petomane alone on the stage, his backside

saying more than his face, the box-office receipts were 20,000 francs.

As a boy Le Petomane, while swimming in the ocean, discovered, purely by accident, that he was able to draw water through his anus into his large intestine. Through exercise of this unique ability he developed a talent for drawing air into his rectum and farting at will. By applying the precise pressure required and by controlling the anal sphincter, he was able to fart tenor, baritone, and bass while rendering simple melodies.

When Le Petomane had perfected this talent, he prepared meticulously for his public debut. He was tall, six feet two inches, with a Wilhelm II moustache, crew-cut hair, and handsome deadpan face. He presented himself in elegant costume —red coat, silk collar, black stockings, patent-leather shoes, white butterfly tie, white gloves, and black satin breeches with a slit up the back.

The billboard at the Moulin Rouge read: "Every evening from 8 to 9, Le Petomane. The only one who pays no author's royalties." At the appointed hour the compere announced, "Le Petomane, a sensational act never before seen or heard." The artist appeared and entertained his audience with some humorous opening remarks in which he explained that Petomane meant someone who can break wind at will. He began the demonstration with a series of small farts, first imitating a little girl, a mother-in-law, a bride on her wedding night, the tearing of cloth, the roar of a cannon, a clap of thunder, and so forth. The audience howled with laughter and responded with unbounded enthusiasm.

Le Petomane inserted the end of a rubber tube through the aperture in the seat of his pants and placed a cigarette in the other end of the tube. He lit the cigarette, inhaled, removed the cigarette, and exhaled a puff of smoke from the end of the tube. After attaching a small six-stop flute to the hose, he played several musical numbers. This was followed by a dazzling array of imitations of domestic and barnyard animals. For the finale he blew out a candle that was placed on a chair some twelve inches from his backside.

Le Petomane, the rage of Paris, became the main attraction at the Moulin Rouge from 1892 to 1914. His fans returned over and over again to be entertained by his ever-expanding variety of impressions, ranging from rapid-firing machine guns to a well-played trombone. In order to prove that no trickery was involved, he performed in the nude for all-male audiences and gave demonstrations for, and was examined by, medical doctors.

Le Petomane, a jolly and simple man who loved to laugh and make others laugh, was a devoted husband and father. Throughout his busy and happy eighty-eight years he was never ill. Few, in their lifetime, have known such fame and popularity. He was always grateful for the gift he had been given and never experienced stage fright in presenting his musical derriere. In the course of his long career, he had given his best.

THE LE PETOMANE PRINCIPLE: If you want people to laugh, it's better to fart than to have no act at all.

THE COWBOY PHILOSOPHER

Will Rogers became famous for his unique blend of humor and common sense. His homespun philosophy and wit made him the most beloved comedian of his day. Hardly a subject escaped his acute attention, but for this interview I decided to question him about the current political situation. Because Will was killed in an airplane crash near Point Barrow, Alaska, on August 15, 1935, his answers to my questions were selected from statements he made during his lifetime.

PETER: Mr. Rogers, why are you so interested in politics?
ROGERS: Politicians can do more funny things naturally than I can think of to do purposely.

PETER: Do you feel that common sense is so scarce that it is seldom a political issue?

ROGERS: Neither is honesty an issue in politics. It's a miracle.

PETER: Why don't we demand more of our political leaders?

ROGERS: No nation likes "hooey" like we do. We are all cuckoo, but we are happy.

PETER: What about all the graft and political payoffs?

ROGERS: Wouldn't it be great if other countries started electing by the ballot instead of the bullet, and us electing by the ballot instead of the bullion?

PETER: Didn't you say that we have the best Congress that money can buy?

ROGERS: Just finished shooting scenes here in Washington for a movie of the old stage play *A Texas Steer*. It was a story of a man elected to Washington on bought votes. We are bringing it up to date by not changing it at all.

PETER: It will not surprise you to hear that the last three elected Presidents were popular at the voting booth, but soon became losers in the popularity polls.

ROGERS: The short memories of American voters is what keeps our politicians in office.

PETER: By poking fun at both political parties are you trying to say something about party politics?

ROGERS: Party politics is the most narrow minded occupation in the world. . . . All you would have to do to make some men Atheists is just tell them the Lord belonged to the opposition Political Party.

PETER: The problems of inflation are still with us. The President's primary problem seems to be his inability to curb inflation.

ROGERS: Last year we said, "Things can't go on like this." And they didn't, they got worse.

PETER: Aren't we blaming the President for a mess he inherited from the Republican administration?

ROGERS: Let's stop blaming the President and the Republicans for all this. Why, they're not smart enough to have thought of all that's happening to us lately.

PETER: What is your opinion of our tax system?

ROGERS: Income tax has made more liars out of the American people than golf has.

PETER: How come?

ROGERS: Even when you make a tax form out on the level, you don't know when it's through if you are a crook or a martyr.

PETER: People always want lower taxes.

ROGERS: People want just taxes more than they want lower taxes. They want to know that every man is paying his proportionate share according to his wealth.

PETER: What about our foreign policy?

ROGERS: We'll show the world we are prosperous, even if we have to go broke to do it.

PETER: Aren't you in favor of helping the underdeveloped countries?

ROGERS: Something ought to be done about these "primitive" people who live in various parts of the world, and don't know a thing but to live off what nature provides. You would think they would get civilized and learn to live off each other like we civilized folks do.

PETER: Could you summarize your attitude toward other countries?

ROGERS: No nation has a monopoly on good things. Each one has something that the others could well afford to adopt.

PETER: If Lincoln were alive today, how would he fare?

ROGERS: Being a Republican he would vote the Democratic ticket. Being in sympathy for the underdog he would be classed as a radical progressive. Having a sense of humor he would be called eccentric.

PETER: You said that you enjoyed Calvin Coolidge.

ROGERS: President Coolidge kept his mouth shut. That was such a novelty among politicians that it just swept the country. Originality will be rewarded in any line.

PETER: Franklin D. Roosevelt tried new ideas. He formed a brain trust.

ROGERS: He said he would take brains anytime in preference to politics. He just as good as admitted you couldn't get both in the same body.

PETER: You seem to delight in making fun of both parties.

ROGERS: If we didn't have two parties, we would all settle on the best men in the country and things would run fine. But as it is, we settle on the worst ones and then fight over 'em.

PETER: You are credited with saying, "I belong to no organized political party. I'm a Democrat."

ROGERS: I keep saying I'm a Democrat, but I ain't. I just pretend to because Democrats are funny and I'm supposed to be.

PETER: Are there any lessons we can learn from past political conventions?

ROGERS: The Republican Convention, 1928, opened with a prayer. If the Lord can see his way clear to bless the Republican Party the way it's been carrying on then the rest of us ought to get blessed without even asking for it.

PETER: Well, what about Democratic conventions?

ROGERS: Always excitement at a Democratic anything! There is always something that will stir up an argument even if they all agree.

PETER: Why are there so many candidates?

ROGERS: Be a politician; no training necessary.

PETER: Do you have any personal political plans?

ROGERS: I am going to jump out some day and be indefinite enough about everything that they will call me a politician, then run on a platform of question marks, and be elected unanimously, then reach in the treasury and bring back my district a new bridge, or tunnel, or dam, and I will be a statesman.

AND HEEEERE'S JOHNNY

As a result of only four appearances on the *Tonight Show*, one of the questions I am asked is: "What is Johny Carson really like?" I am naturally flattered to be regarded as an expert on a question of such widespread and intense interest —a question that piques the curiosity of Carson watchers and evokes the imaginative speculations of gossip columnists. Finding that an honest answer, "How should I know? I was only a guest on the program," did not satisfy my questioners, I decided to provide myself with some better answers.

In the first place, Johnny Carson is the best in a relatively new role, that is as the host of a national-comedy-entertainment-talk-television show. Radio and television have presented interview programs upon which news and serious matters have been discussed. Variety entertainment has been presented as a series of acts on such programs as the Milton Berle, Garry Moore, and Ed Sullivan shows. In contrast, the *Tonight Show*, along with its imitators, is a comedy program with interviews and variety acts, musicians, actors, starlets, singers, and dancers, with an occasional scholar thrown in for uncomic relief.

Johnny Carson has become so closely identified with the *Tonight Show*, in the minds of his viewers, that a discussion of one without the other would make very little sense. To find the equivalent of this contemporary ritualistic television program, we have to go back to the last century. The design of the *Tonight Show* has its roots in an early and uniquely American entertainment, the minstrel show. By the middle of the last century the minstrel show had adopted a standard format. The performance was presided over by the interlocutor, who throughout the show sat in the center position onstage. Much of the comedy was provided by the banter between the interlocutor and two end men—Mr. Tambo and Mr. Bones, who wore outlandish costumes, in contrast with the interlocutor's more conservative garb. These three provided the permanent structure of the show with the other entertainers seated in a row on either side of the interlocutor.

Television has imposed some minor modifications on this format to accommodate the need for commercials and the limitations of the camera. Because the TV screen is small, most of the time the camera must focus on one person or a small group. Therefore, in television it would be useless to arrange the entertainers symetrically on either side of the stage. For the same reason, both end men, Ed McMahon and Doc Severinsen, need not dress in gaudy raiment. By having only Doc dress in wild multicolored outfits, Johnny can direct all his clothing jokes at Doc and all his drinking jokes at Ed.

Within this structure, four nights a week (formerly five)

Johnny Carson demonstrates to millions of viewers that he is the grand master of television hosts.

Following Ed's introduction, "And now . . . heeeere's Johnny! Hi—Yoooo," Johnny steps from behind the curtain and, before his monologue is over, has once again established himself as king of late-night television.

Before the camera, Johnny is the model of middle-class elegance. Greeted by applause, he raises his hand to quiet the audience and remarks, "I know, I know, I felt the same way when I first saw the Statue of Liberty." When a joke fails to get a laugh, he may turn to Ed, point at the audience, and say, "Look, see how quickly they turn on you." This ability to rescue a failing punch line is Johnny's greatest strength as a comedian. When Johnny is on the show, it has a spirit of spontaneity, even in its rehearsed routines, that is missing when guest hosts take over. This improvisational quality, his boyish personality, his acceptability by a broad spectrum of viewers, his modesty and self-deprecation, his involvement of his audience, his ability to recover when jokes fail, his comedic talent, and his consistent embracing of humanitarian causes have all contributed to his phenomenal success.

How did a small-town boy born in Corning, Iowa, become America's Prince of Darkness? When he was thirteen, he sent away for a magic kit in order to amaze and mystify his friends. After long and hard practice he mastered the tricks and soon was performing for pay at service clubs, local fairs, and festivals. He started his radio career in Lincoln, Nebraska, and in 1951 moved to California, where he talked himself into a staff announcer's job at station KNXT. It was here that he created his own show *Carson's Cellar*.

On October 1, 1962, he became the host of the *Tonight Show*. From that day on Johnny Carson became one of the best-known and least-known men in America.

In conclusion I must confess that I am not a completely

objective observer. Johnny Carson and the *Tonight Show* have been very good to me. The four appearances on the show helped sell my books, but not appearing on the show has also helped me. As well as the four appearances I made in front of the camera, I made four appearances at the studio when I had been notified to report to NBC, went to makeup, was assigned a dressing room, waited in the green room, and then was told that my appearance was canceled because the show was running overtime. On these occasions I was paid for showing up and doing nothing. In every other job, I had to do something or they didn't pay me anything. Getting paid for doing nothing was the fulfillment of a lifetime dream. I so wanted this to continue that I told Johnny I was available for cancellation on a continuing basis. That was my last appearance on the *Tonight Show*.

A COMEDIAN FOR ALL SEASONS

"Did you ever notice that there aren't many Chinese guys named Rusty?" That observation was made by George Carlin, a comedian with a talent for the thought-provoking comment, "I just thought of the perfect crime. You pick one guy up by the ankles, and you kill another guy with him. They both die, and there's no murder weapon. The police will probably think it was a pedestrian accident."

I first met George Carlin back in 1972. I was looking forward to a scheduled appearance on the *Dick Cavett Show* and to being interviewed by Cavett. When I arrived in New York, I was told that George Carlin was hosting the show for the night of my appearance.

Never having seen Carlin in the role of interviewer, I wondered what I was in for. Back in the sixties I had seen him do his spoofs of pop radio by performing comic impressions of a disc jockey, sports announcer, newscaster, and

weatherman. In these skits he wore a conservative business suit, had short hair and the general appearance of the bright, clean-cut young man who would have middle-class acceptance. His act was hilarious as he rolled his eyes and mugged his way through the various characters he created for his imaginary radio station Wonderful WINO, 1750 on your dial.

As a slightly demented broadcaster he introduced the news with:

Good evening, ladies and gentlemen. Once again the little hand is on four, the big hand is on two, and it's time for the six o'clock report.

This was followed by news items such as:

A man has barricaded himself inside his house. However, he was not armed, and no one paid any attention.

In labor news, longshoremen walked off the piers today; rescue operations are continuing!

Well, the world breathes a little easier today as five more nations have signed a nuclear test-ban treaty. Today's signers were Chad, Sierra Leone, Upper Volta, Monaco, and Iceland.

Barry Goldwater has definitely decided to be a candidate in '64. He will campaign in all thirteen states.

Wonderful WINO also featured sports announcer Biff Burns:

And quickly now, the basketball scores: 110–108, 126–114, 131–109. And here's a partial score—Boston 58.

A favorite character was the hippy, dippy weatherman, Al Sleet:

Hey, baby, what's happening? Tonight's forecast is . . . dark.

Although Carlin was a big hit with this material by 1969, he was caught up in the times and, after a brief withdrawal from the show scene, emerged as a bearded, long-haired, rock-culture comic clad in a gray T-shirt and jeans. The content of his comedy now included the drug scene, censorship, the war, and other topics of concern to the young.

How would the new counterculture Carlin handle the job of hosting a talk show intended for a large nationwide TV audience? The answer to that was: "Very well." His humor was successful, and his questioning brought out the best in each guest. So far I had seen three different Carlins; the clean-cut wisecracker, the long-haired protest comic, and the highly intelligent, sensitive, and competent interviewer.

My curiosity was aroused. Why had he changed his performance style so abruptly? What motivated him to give up success with one type of comedy for an uncertain future with another? When I attempted to answer these questions, this is what I found.

George Carlin was born in 1937 to Irish Catholic parents and grew up on the Upper West Side of New York City. When he thinks about his childhood, he remembers being alone a lot of the time. He credits being a loner to his early interest in comedy. At an early age he became a mimic and filled his solitary hours playing a variety of personalities.

When he went to school, he found that the classroom provided him with an audience for his clowning. He discovered that he could produce strange sounds that delighted his classmates. He practiced eye movements until he could roll his eyes in different directions, and he made many different funny faces. Today, looking back on his school days, he says that the classroom is the best place for the beginning comic because education is supposed to be so serious. There is so much suppressed laughter that all the class clown has to do is trigger its release by making a funny face, sound, or comment. So, when George became bored with the lesson, he'd say to himself, "Why not deprive someone else of their education?"

At seventeen he joined the Air Force and was sent to Barksdale Air Force Base at Shreveport. He planned to study radio when his tour of duty was over so he could become a disc jockey. But according to George, he got lucky while still in the service. He found that by hanging around a radio station, he eventually got a chance to go on the air because the managers knew cheap labor when they saw it. Between records he started developing the voices and characters he used later in his comedy routines. When out of the service, he continued working as a DJ in Shreveport for a year and then moved on to similar jobs in Boston and Fort Worth.

It was in Fort Worth that he met an old friend, Jack Burns (who later became the partner of Avery Schreiber). As the team Burns and Carlin they appeared in coffeehouses and nightclubs. In only seven months after the team was formed they were on the Jack Paar television show. The team did fairly well for two years but broke up in 1962, when George returned to New York. It was here he started his career as a single at the Café au Go Go.

His big break came with an appearance on the *Merv Griffin Show* in 1965. Other television shows followed, and in 1966 he became the summer replacement for John Davidson. It was during this period that George presented himself as the squeaky-clean impressionist and topical jokester.

In 1969 he felt a need to examine who he was and what he was doing. He withdrew his establishment type of comedy act. He left the nightclub scene totally. He reappeared as the long-haired, bearded, T-shirted, freewheeling, hip counter-culture comedian. With this new approach he became a solid concert performer in theaters and colleges. Recordings of his performances became enduring best sellers.

Today his comedy includes some of the earlier type of news item:

> Police fired guns over the heads of rioters. However, they killed two hundred people living on the second floor.
> Out at the lake today police arrested a one-armed man who was bothering other boaters by continuously rowing in a circle.
> Scientists have just discovered a cure for apathy. However, no one has shown the slightest interest.

His basic material, though, still causes us to question our values and customs. On his latest tour he has been doing a routine on death and dying that is hilariously funny while it brings into question all our delusive language on the subject. Recently he has placed more emphasis on the little things that keep us together rather than the big things that keep us apart.

Although I found out many things about George Carlin, he is still an enigma, a constantly changing serious thinker who juggles the contradictions of our society for humorous effect. Three things keep him moving, and as long as they are in operation, he will continue to be one of our most relevant and effective comedians: (1) Once he feels that a routine is perfected he records it and then develops new material. (2) Words are his work, his play, his passion, and he keeps questioning our use of words. (3) He remains open to the things that surprise and delight him and maintain his interest in the ironic and the absurd.

CHAPTER 4

A Woman's Place

PETER'S SEXIST PRINCIPLE: Most hierarchies were established by men who now occupy the upper levels, thus depriving women of an equal opportunity to achieve their own levels of incompetence.

THROUGHOUT THE AGES, SLY MATRIARCHS OF THE WORLD have twisted the nominal monarchs and politicos around their pretty, bejeweled fingers. They have inspired and initiated the falls of kings, heads, and countries with their wit and cleverness. Back in nineteenth-century France, Madame Germaine de Staël gave Napoleon Bonaparte more than upper abdominal gas pains with her wit, and Madame Récamier made history from her chaise lounge.

No man can be held throughout the day by what happens throughout the night.

—SALLY STANFORD

In the days when the socially acceptable female role was to flatter and support the male ego, women writers of humor were inclined to be rather sneaky about it. They seemed to be writing for women about women. Not only are the novels of Jane Austen treasures of subtle humor, but much of it is at the expense of the men in her stories. Her male contemporaries, it appears, regarded this domestic humor as trivia and in typical chauvinistic fashion concluded that women were incapable of real wit. This was to be expected since to admit the existence of female wit would be to admit that man was its victim.

A woman has to be twice as good as a man to go half as far.

—FANNIE HURST

In the New World, feminists Elizabeth Cady Stanton, Lucretia Mott, and Susan B. Anthony used effective and scathing podium wit to change the course of history by establishing the fight for women's rights as an ongoing movement in America. Paralleling the early fight for women's rights and the present feminist movement, women humorists have been taking over more space for themselves on the nation's bookshelves, yet the number of works that reflect the changes in sexual attitudes are limited.

Woman's virtue is man's greatest invention.

—CORNELIA OTIS SKINNER

Fifty years ago it was said that there was no room at the Algonquin Round Table for anyone who could not, at the drop of a bon mot, coin an epigram. Few were as facile as Dorothy Parker. Alexander Woollcott deemed the demure-appearing Mrs. Parker "a combination of little Nell and Lady Macbeth." Her judgment of women writers was, perhaps, premature: "It's a terrible thing to say, but I can't think of good women writers. Of course, calling them women writers is their ruin; they begin to think of themselves that way."

Reviewing one book, she wrote: "This is not a novel to be tossed aside lightly. It should be thrown with great force." She gave this advice to a friend whose sick cat had to be put away: "Try curiosity." Describing a guest at one of her parties, she said, "That woman speaks eighteen languages but can't say 'No' in any of them." On hearing that President Coolidge was dead, she asked, "How can you tell?" She once claimed that her dog had caught a social disease from using a public lamppost. When asked why she named her canary Onan, she explained, "Because it spills its seed upon the ground." Her caustic whimsicality, ready tongue, and mastery of the verbal put-down won her many fans among the admirers of wit and helped change our expectations of women humorists.

I don't care what people do as long as they don't do it in the streets and scare the horses.
—MRS. PATRICK CAMPBELL

Today we have television and movie stars Lily Tomlin, Phyllis Diller, and Joan Rivers, who are also writers of humor, and among the growing number of comedy writers for television we have the energetic Susan Harris, who not only writes but also produces and directs the successful comedy *Soap*.

This is the second time I have performed in Toronto, not counting my honeymoon.
—CAROL LAWRENCE

The number of she-wits has grown, and the variety of subjects they write about has increased, but two types of humor have had few female practitioners. First, published female cartoonists are a rarity, and of these only a very few have ever achieved regular national syndication. Secondly, the number of women writers who have used satire as the means of dealing with major issues and exposing flaws in our major institutions is quite limited.

In days gone by,
the maids were shy,
and went about with downcast eye.
Now maids are bold
and wear socks rolled,
and men cast down their eyes, I'm told.
—COLETTE BURNS

NO NOSE FOR SUCCESS

Why are there so few women cartoonists? Cartoons and comic strips appeal to males and females of all ages. Cartoonists deal with subject matter in every area from the domestic scene to the political arena. Humorous women newspaper and magazine writers have been with us for a long time, but where have the women cartoonists been?

Most of the cartoon strips about females have been created by men. Someday I hope to find the reason for this, but in the meantime, we can look at the career of one female cartoonist and see if we can find some clues.

There is a nationally syndicated comic strip called *Cathy* because Cathy is the central character in the strip. Cathy is also the name of the artist who writes and draws the cartoon. Although the strip is largely autobiographical, it is easy to distinguish between the real-life Cathy and the cartoon-strip Cathy. A careful examination of their pictures will reveal that the cartoon Cathy has no nose and the real Cathy has.

Thus, cartoon Cathy has a nothing profile, requiring that she face the reader directly and make all her sideways glances through eye movements alone, while real Cathy has a very beautiful profile and has no unusual limitations in her head movements.

Now that we have established a positive means of differentiation between the two Cathys, let us direct our attention first to the cartoon Cathy. She first appeared on the national scene as a syndicated strip nearly three years ago and already is a feature in 125 newspapers, and the number is growing.

Cathy strikes a responsive chord in us because of her humanness and vulnerability. Her problem is one to which we can relate, that of coping with the changing values and conflicts created by living in the seventies.

Cathy is a plump young woman in a thin world. Her large, expressive eyes reflect her moods. Her long, straight blond hair provides instant identification. She wears a heart high on the center of her ill-fitting sweater that reveals no sign of a bustline. In spite of her lack of the qualities of traditional feminine beauty, she is instantly appealing.

In each strip, Cathy is confronted by her own ambivalence and the confusion of our times. Andrea, her closest friend and alter ego, is an unrelenting feminist and crusader for Women's Lib, who urges Cathy to be self-sufficient and assertive. Yet, try as she may to be independent, Cathy is inhibited by the traditional values of her upbringing. Intellectually she accepts the principles of Women's Lib, but when she tries to put them into practice, she has difficulty carrying them through. Her conviction of the rightness of her struggle for independence from male domination is in conflict with her desire for male companionship, love, and even protection. She summarizes her position on the issue in her most quoted line: "It's boring to be invincible all by yourself."

Her boyfriend, Irving, is not much help. He is an egotist who says he understands her problems, but his behavior is obnoxious and shows a lack of understanding. For Valentine's Day he suggested that Cathy pick out her own card. He lets her do his laundry, watches the programs he wants on her TV, and then dates other women. She hates being treated this way but hangs onto him because she feels he is a challenge.

Cathy has similar conflicts on other issues. She tries to diet but loves to eat. Even when she is anxious about her weight, she consoles herself with food. She orders a hamburger with french fries and a milk shake but feels virtuous because she doesn't eat the bun. She concludes one strip, in which she finds her clothes getting tight, with: "Never put your jeans in the dryer the day after you've pigged out at McDonald's." In another she begins by telling Andrea how much she likes the new labeling on a cereal box that says it has only eighty-eight calories per serving. After she has served herself half the box, Andrea points out that the label also states there are supposed to be twenty servings per package. Upon hearing this, Cathy does one of her typical reversals and concludes, "I hate this stupid labeling!" Her life is filled with imponderables, like the time she tried to get a suntan, but her legs stayed white, and her nose turned red. She asked the unanswerable question "How can the sun keep passing up something so big to get to something so small?"

Real-life Cathy Guisewite grew up in the Midwest, surrounded by a creative and supportive family. Her father has his own advertising agency, and her mother was also in advertising until the children were born.

After graduating from the University of Michigan, with a degree in English, Cathy followed in her parents' footsteps and went into advertising as a copywriter for a Detroit agency. She was so competent that it wasn't long before she was vice-president of the company.

When writing home to her parents, Cathy illustrated her letters with stick-figure drawings showing scenes from her life in Detroit. These sketches expressed her humorous view of

her problems and anxieties. Her mother saved the drawings and urged her reluctant daughter to submit them for publication. The publishing syndicate responded affirmatively to her writing but suggested that she improve her artwork. In seven months of experimental doodling and study of self-help guidebooks, she taught herself to draw acceptable cartoons. The strip made its publishing debut on November 22, 1976.

Cathy Guisewite continued to work at the agency by day and draw the cartoon strip at night and on weekends, but eventually doing both became too much. She quit the advertising business and became a full-time cartoonist. Now she completes and sends in four weeks of cartoons for daily and Sunday papers in one batch, spending about two hours on each daily strip and five hours on each Sunday block. Her procedure is to spend many days writing and then to do all of the drawings.

At twenty-seven, Cathy is a slender, beautiful brown-eyed brunette. Her living quarters and studio are in her condominium in Southfield, Michigan, where she lives alone with her dog, Trolley. She enjoys her work and the financial independence it has brought her. She is only the second woman to achieve nationwide prominence in the male world of comics, joining Brenda Starr's creator, Dale Messick.

Cathy says that one reason she writes the comic strip is that she resents the *Vogue* image of the cool, slick, impervious "bionic" woman, to whom the average female can't help comparing herself unfavorably. The question asked of her most frequently is how autobiographical is the strip. She admits that many of the comic-strip Cathy's problems are her own. She is torn between living the traditional role of women and being more assertive and independent. When comic Cathy is like that, it is a reflection of her own life. She also gets ideas from observing her friends and from reading advice-to-the-lovelorn columns and feminist publications. Whatever her source, she presents us with humor that reminds us of our own reality.

Now that she is a celebrity she is invited to lecture and to be a TV talk-show guest. Once she was asked how she felt about being interviewed on television. She said, "I'm both excited and terrified. It's too much to try to look good, laugh, and be entertaining at the same time."

THREE JEERS FOR BUREAUCRACY

Most books and articles satirizing bureaucracy ridicule its nonresponsiveness to real needs. Few satirists explore beyond the effects of bureaucracy and probe beneath the surface to show the meaning of what is actually happening. One exception to this is Joseph Heller's novel *Catch-22*,[10] a hilariously grotesque military fantasy. In fulfilling their responsibilities to the bureaucracy, Heller's characters carry out senseless, lethal assignments that appear to be essentially similar to those in real situations. In so doing, they reveal a dehumanized world of hypocrisy and greed. Beneath the surface of this mad farce lurks the question "Who is sane in a world whose major energies are devoted to blowing itself up?"

This is satire in the grand tradition. It employs irony, derision, and wit to expose folly and point out major inconsistencies in our behavior. A satirical work of this magnitude may appear only once in a lifetime, but I am still on the lookout for fresh bureaucratic satire.

Recently my quest was rewarded when I received a little book from India, *3 Jeers for Bureaucracy*.[11] It describes how the various departments of the Indian government are administered so as to serve the needs of career bureaucrats rather than to provide public service.

Interested as I was in the subject matter of the book, I was equally interested in the author. Rama Sinha is a young woman who describes herself as an engineer by profession, a bureaucrat through association, and a writer by aspiration. She grew up in Bombay, Delhi, Ranchi, and other places where her father had been posted as a government engineer. In 1965 she graduated from Roorkee University with a degree in electronic engineering. She has been a college lecturer and is presently working in an electronics company in Chandigarh, where she lives with her husband and ten-year-old son. Although a woman and an engineer, she claims that it was neither the Lib nor the Lab that brought her to the subject of bureaucracy, but simply her observations and experience in coping with government hierarchies.

The book is presented as a straightforward manual for operating the bureaucracy, but the author places her tongue in her cheek whenever she finds a bureaucrat putting his foot in his mouth. In defending the need for critical examination of bureaucracy, she says, "We cannot do without bureaucracy, but let not bureaucracy try again to do without us."

I have been impressed with the similarity of bureaucracies in a number of countries with different cultures and with governments of diametrically opposed political philosophies. A touch of bureaucracy makes the whole world kin. With this thought in mind let us see what Rama Sinha has to say about Indian bureaucracy.

The Metamorphosis of Bureaucracy

The essence of bureaucracy lies in the character of the bureaucrat. The bureaucrat and bureaucracy are so intricately related that it is difficult to say which is the painter and which the picture. A bureaucrat is what bureaucracy makes him, and bureaucracy is what the bureaucrat makes of it.

Bureaucracy continues to be the fundamental factor in government administration. Departments work through a chain of bureaucratic technocrats who are heads of their respective blocks and who become known as blockheads. Although "official" power is directly related to the position on the hierarchy, bureaucratic importance and administrative impotence are mathematically related: The higher the hierarchy, the greater the impotence.

The Image of a Bureaucrat

A bureaucrat may be seen as a perverse god who must be served, a benevolent despot, a recalcitrant ass that must be driven, a cowardly bully, or even a hardworking, underpaid, harassed official doing his best under difficult circumstances. Some etymologically minded analysts have suggested that the word "bureaucrat" is a distorted version of the word "burrow-rat," meaning that he is not the owner of a bureau but the occupant of a burrow. Facile speech, mod attire, and behavioral hypocrisy are the trademarks of today's bureaucrat.

His attitude toward his job is characterized by intense apathy. He is a stickler for rules and a fondler of procedures; he behaves like an accountant without the mental approach of a finance manager. He is ever ready to propose solutions but unable to pinpoint problems.

His ambition is to be always on the right side of power, and he aspires only to be a favored follower. His is the classic stoop to success. Promotion is the motivation behind a bureaucrat's survival; it keeps him pegged between the two choices of hands-up and pants-down.

The New Process of Decision Making

The traditional process of decision making involved (1) fact collection, (2) data analysis, (3) objective formulation, and (4) decision by the competent authority. The new bureaucratic process is much more complex because it must keep the hierarchy intact and involves (1) anticipating what the boss wants, (2) if one cannot anticipate, waiting for further directions, (3) if they are not forthcoming, following recommendations, (4) if these fail to guide one, invoking intuitive judgment, and (5) if this yields nothing, as often happens, calling for precedents.

Three levels of decision making within a bureaucracy have been identified:

1. THE DECISION-INVOKING LEVEL. At this level the bureaucrat who has been presented with a file requiring a decision directs the file upward with a request for the superior's decision.

2. DECISION-PROVOKING LEVEL. At this level, which is below that of Number 1 above, the bureaucrat assembles the facts, comments, grievances, and so forth and directs the file upward for perusal.

3. THE DECISION-CHOKING LEVEL. At this level the bureaucrat's job is to subject the file to the mass of tangled and conflicting rules assembled to assure that any considered nondecision is politically acceptable, technically feasible, legally correct, administratively suitable, and so on.

The Sutras (aphoristic doctrinal summaries) of Success

There are two objectives in hearing public grievance: (1) to make the complaint vanish or (2) to make the complainant vanish. The first is usually beyond the competence of the bureaucrat, but the second is well within his area of responsibility. The complaint cannot exist without the complainant, and if the complainant does not exist, the complaint automatically vanishes.

Make the boss happy and the subordinates afraid. Remember that it is the boss who can open the door that leads to the top and that a subordinate is like a drum; the harder you hit, the better the effect.

Keep the file perfect and the mind empty. The more one fills the file, the more one empties the mind. Once a thing goes into the file there is neither the justification nor the necessity for carrying its burden in the mind. A perfect file may carry the evidence of many a faux pas, and the record of many a failing of others, that are essential to the success seeker. Also, the empty mind is the bureaucrat's workshop in which he can discover the ever more perfect way of keeping the file.

Don't get caught. The only thing worse than getting caught in an unworthy act is the admission of it. What is relevant is not what one is, but whether one is caught in what one is. A thief is one who is caught; a crook is one who is found out; corruption is that which is discovered; favoritism is that which is proved. Therefore, do not hesitate to keep conduct below and records above board. Do anything, but don't get caught.

WINNING THE RAT RACE WITHOUT BECOMING A RAT

If eighteenth-century essayists Joseph Addison and Sir Richard Steele could peer over the tops of their glasses at the latest issue of their still popular London journal *The Spectator*, they would probably flip their respective wigs. In an era in which women were treated with either false chivalry or outright contempt, Addison and Steele admired and respected women as human beings every bit as capable as men.

The writing team of Addison and Steele, who parted this realm some 250 years ago, has come once more to our attention—or at least their names have. A twentieth-century woman writer and book editor applauded their sentiment toward women and adopted the pseudonym Addison Steele in their honor.

In her book *Upward Nobility, How to Win the Rat Race Without Becoming a Rat*,[12] Ms. Steele includes a statement from *The Spectator* (July 30, 1714) by Addison and Steele that expresses her philosophy: "A man should always consider how much he has more than he wants, and how much more unhappy he might be than he really is."

Her ideas are in contrast with popular contemporary self-help volumes, such as Michael Korda's *Success!*, Michael Maccoby's *The Gamesman,* and Robert Ringer's *Looking Out for Number 1* and *Winning Through Intimidation*, that resemble combat manuals for fighting your way to the top of the heap. In counterpoint to this kind of savage career advice, Addison Steele tells us about her friends in the publishing world, how they were trapped into playing corporate management's game, and how they sacrificed their own happiness, life-style, and personality to the ambition of superiors dedicated to the solemn nine-to-five ritual of worship of the bottom line.

The Company's Chessboard

Her comments about corporate mindset (or mindlessness set) remind us that no matter how tailored the suit, opulent the suite, or crisp the speech, management is not too far removed from the mores of the robber barons. For the most part, it would appear that large numbers of those in the rat race are not only scratching for a living but clawing their way up a slippery ladder of success made hazardous by droppings from those above on the rungs below.

The corporate clones that control the hierarchal process have a vast array of tricks with which to beguile the unwary. At the outset we are reminded that a business organization exists to make money, and one of its goals is to get the most work out of you for the lowest amount of money possible. This is not to say that many companies are not pleasant to work for, but the fact remains that businesses do not exist to make their employees happy, or to provide love, recognition, or exciting times.

Companies will motivate a climber with nonmonetary rewards, such as a key to the executive washroom, where rulers may go but where commoners may not venture. Status symbols such as a corner office, permission to eat in the executive dining room, or a company credit card are popular bait. Companies that hand out these low-cost inducements instead of fatter paychecks are confident that people will work harder, compete more fiercely, and symbolically kill to obtain such recognition.

Although lip service is paid by the company to teamwork, corporate hierarchies are set up to encourage competition, not cooperation. For example, a small pool of copywriters has been working cooperatively when the supervisor assigns one job to several writers. The supervisor's bias is the criterion for evaluating which writer gets the nod of approval. Fine for the company, but abrasive and stressful to the rest of the writers. If someone should get fired from that writing team, those still employed will inevitably feel a collective guilt along with relief that "thank God it was another and not me!"

Beating Words into Ployshares

The successful office politician is always in the right place at the right time, with the right ploy or stratagem. It appears that some ploymen have instinctive knowledge of the best buttons to push on the boss's switchboard. A second type plays politics just for the fun of it, delighting in manipulating people by implanting just a snippet of fear.

"I hear the boss is angling for that hotshot art director," he will say in passing. "You know, the one at Burton, Beaten, Bitten, and Shy. The one who got raves for his handling of the Zip account."

This remark, designed to set your mental and emotional wheels in motion, implies that you may be replaced. In reality there may not have been any hotshot art director or any problem. But there is a problem—now.

The third kind of ployman is one who creates the impression that he is convinced he is going to lose. This player has so many complaints that he may appear paranoid, thereby arousing your sympathy. But he will drain your energy, waste your time, and drag you down while he is actually winning the rat race.

A fourth type is the ployman who devotes his energies to creating his image of devoted, loyal, industrious company man. This stance may be exhausting to the office politician and transparent to his coworkers, who may view his efforts with tolerant amusement until raises, promotions, and stock options roll around.

"Look, there goes Ployman taking work home again!" Ployman stops for just a moment outside the boss's office to re-adjust his burden and smile a good-night greeting. Next morning you can be sure that he will bring it to the boss's attention that he finished that work assignment "last night."

Then there's the old lunch-at-the-desk scene, staged, of course, when the boss has to work through his lunch hour. Or the night-school gambit where courses are taken to achieve greater skill and efficiency "for the company's benefit."

Command Performances

Perhaps more insidious than any of the other ploys is the one where the boss or supervisor wants to buddy up with the team after a day's work, for the 5:10 cocktail. If he asks you, and you decline to go, you will not become an intimate and will probably be overlooked when promotion and raises come around. You can count on the office politician's being there with his shoeshine kit, lick, spittle, and all.

In this conflict situation you are damned if you do and condemned if you don't. How do you value your integrity or sense of self when after a day's work you do not need another meeting? How much is *your* time really worth?

Up the Hierarchy

Ms. Steele is aware of the potential danger of turning down a promotion. The boss may be offended if you turn down his offer to head up the Dirty Didy Expungement Division, some Siberia of activity that no one wants. After all, he is offering you more authority, a corner office, a company car, and a title. These are things he values. He may think there is something wrong with you if you don't think they're wonderful, too.

There are subtle ways for turning down promotion. "I still have so much to learn about my present job before I could consider . . ." or "It's certainly not up to me to make suggestions, but I happen to know that Kitty Litter, in research, did a study of detergents and would be well qualified for the Dirty Didy Division."

Addison Steele brings a message of hope to the moderate achievers of the world. The good life is yours for the having if you learn to avoid the pitfalls of the corporate life. If you are always angling for the next rung on the ladder, how can you possibly ever enjoy the view from the rung you are on?

Assuming you are a nice person who does not want to spend your life locking horns with others, pretending friendships you do not feel, or, conversely, abandoning friends you like so as to further your advancement, you are one of the Upward Nobility who may survive the rat race without becoming a rat.

Steele's Laws

Many of Addison Steele's observations relating to promotion, office politics, memos, and estimates are expressed as laws.

STEELE'S FIRST LAW: It is easier never to go forward than to have to go backward.

Corollary: You will have to learn how to turn down promotions except the ones you've chosen to make your job more rewarding.

Corollary: It is better to make sure you are never offered a promotion you don't want than to have to turn it down.

STEELE'S SECOND LAW: Not everyone plays politics to get ahead.

Corollary: Some people simply like the game of politics.

STEELE'S THIRD LAW: More people write memos than read them.

Corollary: If people stopped writing memos completely, very few people would notice.

STEELE'S FOURTH LAW: Memos are never written for the person to whom they are addressed.

Corollary: Unless you keep a copy of your own memo for future protection, there is no point in writing it in the first place.

Corollary: Memos will be sent to as many people as the memo writer can think of.

STEELE'S FIFTH LAW: Proceed on the assumption that all estimates are meaningless.

Corollary: Proceed on the assumption that everyone around you is proceeding on the assumption that all estimates are meaningless.

Corollary: Even if you yourself provide others with the most scrupulously accurate projections, everyone around you will be proceeding on the assumption that your estimates are meaningless.

STEELE'S SIXTH LAW: No matter how much money a company is making, it always thinks it should be making more.

CHAPTER 5

Take Me to Your Leader

I DON'T WRITE ABOUT POLITICS. I WOULD IF I COULD, BUT I just can't decide which side I should be on. After studying many political issues I wrote:

> *PETER'S POLITICAL RULE: There are two sides to every issue—and both sides are wrong.*

Although I do not write about politics, I am interested in the people in politics. For example, my study of American Presidents has taught me a lot.

From Warren Harding I learned that a playboy could be President.

From Calvin Coolidge I learned that one doesn't have to say anything to become President.

From Herbert Hoover I learned that one doesn't have to be a politician to become President.

From Franklin D. Roosevelt I learned that one can make the presidency a lifetime job.

From Harry S. Truman I learned that anyone can be President.

From Dwight Eisenhower I learned that you don't have to do anything to be President.

From John F. Kennedy I learned that a Catholic can become President.

From Lyndon Johnson I learned that it is dangerous to have a President.

From Richard Nixon I learned that a three-time loser could become President and still be a loser.

From Gerald Ford I learned that one can become President with just one vote and nobody will ask for a recount.

From Jimmy Carter I learned that the President can be elected to the White House but have all of his success at Camp David.

There is nothing new in making light of the lives of politicians. The Chinese poet Su Tung-po (A.D. 1036–1101) wrote:

On the Birth of His Son

Families, when a child is born
Want it to be intelligent.
I, through intelligence,
Having wrecked my whole life,
Only hope the baby will prove
Ignorant and stupid.
Then he will crown a tranquil life
By becoming a Cabinet Minister.

One politician whose words I admire is not well known nationwide. The late James McSheehy was a supervisor in San Francisco for twenty-four years until his retirement in 1941. When the city was considering buying six gondolas for a lagoon in Golden Gate Park, McSheehy asked, "Gentlemen, why spend so much? Why not just buy two of them and let nature take its course?" At another meeting at City Hall he said, "This has all the earmarks of an eyesore." His phrases were picturesque, and his logic was whimsical, as demonstrated in these samples: "This comes within a few pennies of being a very large amount"; "We must put our shoulders to the wheel and push the ship of state up Market Street." When he was shown a new hydroelectric plant, he asked, "Do you mean to tell me the people of San Francisco are drinking water after all the electricity has been taken out of it?"

Of his own record at City Hall, McSheehy said, "I may have missed a committee meeting now and then and been late occasionally to our Monday meetings, but no one, sir, can say that I've ever been incumbent"; "Indeed, if there's anything behind this that your humble servant can undercover, I'm going to undercover it."

As chairman of the finance committee he addressed a delegation, "Ladies, I have here some figures which I want you to take home in your heads, which I know are concrete."

Some of his more philosophical utterances were: "Along the invisible pathway to the future, I see the footprints of a hidden hand"; "The roosters have come home to hatch"; "Let's call a shovel a shovel, no matter who we hit." And finally, some good advice for all of us: "You can't straddle the fence and still keep your ear to the ground."

The four leaders that follow—Franklin, Nixon, Stevenson, and Boren—directly or indirectly are sources of humor, no matter how seriously we take their contribution to the political life of America.

Benjamin Franklin's accomplishments are greatly admired, but it is his proverbs and witty sayings that keep his character alive in most people's hearts.

Richard M. Nixon was not the intended focus of the next piece, although he was the object under discussion. A few days after Nixon resigned from the presidency, I wrote a spoof about psychohistorians. In the article I gave my psychological explanation for Nixon's apparently irrational behavior of engaging in dirty tricks to win an election that he already had in the bag. Although my purpose was to satirize psychohistorians for psychoanalyzing famous persons by remote control, it appears that most of my readers mistakenly thought it was intended to make fun of Nixon. That is why this article, which is really about psychological diagnosis, appears in this chapter about leaders rather than in the one about psychology, where it truly belongs. It is also included here because although it was written in jest some time ago, the events in Nixon's recent career have proved my diagnosis to be correct.

Adlai Stevenson is the subject of an interview for one reason only. His answers are witty and eloquent.

James H. Boren ran for President, but that is not why he is included. Boren is a new kind of leader. As president of the only international organization of professional bureaucrats he ridicules the undesirable characteristics of bureaucrats by humorously extolling these characteristics as virtues.

The inner spirit of bureaucracy lies in the exciting interplay of nonideas and the effervescent sparkling of human personalities engaged in nondirective pursuits.
—JAMES H. BOREN

LITTLE STROKES FELL GREAT OAKS

Now that America has passed its two hundredth birthday, I thought it would be worthwhile to talk with the most colorful and versatile member of the signers of the Declaration of Indepndence. Benjamin Franklin excelled as a philosopher, statesman, writer, scientist, inventor, printer, and publisher, while maintaining an active social life and earning a reputation as a notorious womanizer. In this interview I attempted to discover if Franklin's words set down during his lifetime are valid today.

PETER: Mr. Franklin, as an important celebrity, you do me great honor by granting this interview.
FRANKLIN: Most people return small favors, acknowledge middling ones, and repay great ones with ingratitude.
PETER: What I mean is that I am grateful for this time from your busy schedule.
FRANKLIN: Remember that time is money.

PETER: I will try not to waste your time.

FRANKLIN: A little neglect may breed mischief: for want of a nail the shoe was lost; for want of a shoe the horse was lost; and for want of a horse the rider was lost.

PETER: Sir, you are quoting yourself. You seem to relish your sayings about carefulness, economy of time, and thrift.

FRANKLIN: Little strokes fell great oaks. He that goes a borrowing goes a sorrowing. Early to bed and early to rise makes man healthy, wealthy and wise. Never leave till tomorrow that which you can do today.

PETER: If brevity be wit, you are certainly a witty man.

FRANKLIN: There's many witty men whose brains can't fill their bellies.

PETER: In your public life do you try to live by the maxims you published in *Poor Richard's Almanack*?

FRANKLIN: I shall never ask, never refuse, nor ever resign an office.

PETER: Well said!

FRANKLIN: Well done is better than well said.

PETER: And in your private life?

FRANKLIN: Often I sat up in my room reading the greatest part of the night, when the book was borrowed in the evening and to be returned early in the morning, lest it should be missed or wanted.

PETER: Sir, you were America's first postmaster general, minister to the French court, and held many other public offices. Looking back on your career, how do you feel?

FRANKLIN: The first mistake in public business is going into it.

PETER: Why?

FRANKLIN: To serve the public faithfully, and at the same time please it entirely, is impracticable.

PETER: What do you say to critics?

FRANKLIN: Don't throw stones at your neighbors if your own windows are glass.

PETER: I see. You feel that the loudest critics are not above criticism themselves.

FRANKLIN: The worst wheel of the cart makes the most noise.

PETER: Why do you think you have critics when you're one of the most admired men in American history?

FRANKLIN: Setting too good an example is a kind of slander seldom forgiven.

PETER: Modesty doesn't appear to be one of your vices.

FRANKLIN: He that falls in love with himself has no rivals.

PETER: You suffer from gout, yet you continue to drink. Why don't you follow your doctor's advice?

FRANKLIN: There are more old Drunkards than old Doctors.

PETER: Have I asked enough personal questions?

FRANKLIN: You may talk too much on the best of subjects.

PETER: You negotiated the final peace treaty with England that ended the Revolutionary War.

FRANKLIN: There never was a good war or a bad peace.

PETER: You have certainly carried out the commissions that were assigned to you. How do you feel about one's duty to country?

FRANKLIN: Duty is not beneficial because it is commended, but is commended because it is beneficial.

PETER: At the signing of the Declaration of Independence on July 4, 1776, you said . . .

FRANKLIN: We must all hang together, or assuredly we shall all hang separately.

PETER: Why do we have so many corrupt politicians and government officials today?

FRANKLIN: It is hard for an empty sack to stand upright.

PETER: How do you view the future of America?

FRANKLIN: In this world nothing is certain but death and taxes. 'Tis easy to see, hard to foresee.

PETER: Do you worry about today's high rate of unemployment?

FRANKLIN: When men are employed, they are best contented; for on the days they worked they were good-natured and cheerful, and, with the consciousness of having done a good day's work, they spent the evening jollily; but on . . . idle days they were mutinous and quarrelsome.

PETER: With all the violence and hatred in the world today do you think that religion has been a failure?

FRANKLIN: If men are so wicked with religion, what would they be without it?

PETER: What would you do differently if you could live your life over?

FRANKLIN: Were it offered to my choice, I should have no objection to a repetition of the same life from its beginning, only asking the advantages authors have in a second edition to correct some faults of the first.

PETER: You have labored long on your autobiography.

FRANKLIN: The next thing most like living one's life over again seems to be a recollection of that life, and to make that recollection as durable as possible by putting it down in writing.

PETER: Can you summarize your philosophy of life in a few words?

FRANKLIN: Enjoy the present hour, be mindful of the past; and neither fear nor wish the approaches of the last.

PETER: What are your feelings about death?

FRANKLIN: Fear not Death; for the sooner we die, the longer we shall be immortal. Wish not so much to live long, as to live well.

PETER: Will you recall for my readers the epitaph you wrote for yourself as a young man when you were ill and fearful that you might be dying?

FRANKLIN: The body of Benjamin Franklin, Printer (like the cover of an old book, its contents torn out and stripped of its lettering and gilding), lies here, food for worms; but the work shall not be lost, for it will (as he believed) appear once more in a new and more elegant edition, revised and corrected by the Author.

WAS NIXON A VICTIM OF THE PETER PRINCIPLE?

Frequently I am asked, "Was Nixon a victim of the Peter Principle?" I never was in favor of impeachment. My studies of American corporate practices showed that while all hierarchies promote individuals to levels of incompetence, they also provide a means of dispose of a chief executive who becomes an embarrassment. Usually a company president who goofs up undergoes a process called percussive sublimation—he is kicked upstairs. The incompetent executive seldom resists this pseudopromotion.

Ever since the seriousness of Watergate became evident, I have advocated that the post of Premier General be established. If Nixon had been promoted to the purely ceremonial position of Premier General, he would now be cutting ribbons, delivering commencement addresses, riding in parades, and carrying out other prestigious but nonadministrative duties. This would have provided America with the advantages of having a full-time working executive branch as well as a ceremonial branch, without the disadvantages of a hereditary monarchy. With the functions of head of state and head of government separated, the President would be relieved of most of the present social obligations of the office, while the Premier General would have nothing but social and ceremonial obligations.

Although it is obvious that promotion would have been superior to impeachment or resignation, my advice did not prevail, and the country was unnecessarily forced to agonize, for many months, over Watergate.

After Mr. Nixon had resigned and his misuse of power had been exposed, the question of why he engaged in this pathological behavior remained unanswered. Psychohistorians have had a field day trying to analyze Richard M. Nixon. Some have attributed his behavior to various kinds of psychosis. Some of his detractors have called him a psychopath, while his supporters have called him pragmatic. I am unable to differentiate between these two diagnoses. Unfortunately none of these attempts at remote-control psychological analysis has offered a satisfactory explanation of why he employed "dirty tricks" in his '72 campaign, when he already had it made. They fail to say why he installed secret devices to record the details of the cover-up, his plotting against the FBI, and his own obscene language, nor do they say why he did not destroy the tapes when the heat was on. Although the psychological experts have failed to say why Nixon engaged in this self-destructive behavior, which led to his downfall, the answer is not very difficult if we review the evidence objectively. Let us go back to 1962. In that year two important events occurred in Nixon's career. He bade farewell to politics with his now famous words to news reporters, "You won't have Nixon to kick around anymore," and he published his first book, *Six Crises*. Throughout the book his obsessive preoccupation with crises was evident. He said, "Crises may indeed be agony but it is the exquisite agony which a man might not want to experience again—yet would not for the world have missed."

In 1972, six days after the Watergate break-in, in a tape-recorded discussion of the cover-up with Haldeman, Nixon referred repeatedly to *Six Crises*. Nixon urged Haldeman to reread it and told him to buy copies for everyone. He referred to it as a great book that reads like a novel. Later Charles Colson admitted to reading the book fourteen times at Nixon's insistence. I have known some pushy authors, but Nixon is the worst. He was still pushing his book ten years after publication. Obviously Nixon's subconscious ambition was to be a best-selling author.

The foundation of Nixon's literary career was crises, and, consciously or subconsciously, after a six-year layoff he was compelled by his literary zeal to get back into the crises business. This need was made perfectly clear in his selection of Spiro T. Agnew as vice-presidential running mate. Soon after occupying the White House, the President and his men got right to work on illegal surveillance operations, bugging teams, surreptitious entries, "deep sixing" of evidence, plumbers' operations, obstruction of justice, perjury, hush money, blackmail, enemies' lists, the secret bombing of Cambodia, the Pentagon spying on the White House, the White House spying on itself, $100,000 in cash to Bebe Rebozo, San Clemente and tax write-offs, using the FBI and CIA and the Justice Department for political purposes, ITT and the milk fund, falsified polls, doctored documents, and forging of past presidential records.

Why did he do it? Why did he tape-record it? Obviously this was his raw material for a forthcoming series of crises epics. This is why he refused to give up the tapes. Even when he was forced, by the Judiciary Committee, to relinquish the tapes, the author in him prevailed, and he refused to release the raw data. He worked around the clock to prepare his own edited version and presented it in book form. As I watched Nixon on television with his printed version of the tapes, I could not help detecting the pride of authorship in the fleeting smile and fond glance each time he pointed to his stack of freshly bound transcripts.

Nixon said that he criticized only those he respected. Could this be his reason for giving members of the press such a bad time? I believe that it was. His hostile posture when dealing with the press was a reaction formation caused by his jealousy of their positions as writers. Recent events support this interpretation. Almost immediately upon arriving at his San Clemente estate, ordinary citizen Richard M. Nixon ordered that his vice-presidential papers, a previous library donation for tax purposes, not be made available until 1985. He entered into negotiations with a publisher for his memoirs and continued his claim of personal ownership of the White House tapes.

Obviously Nixon was a victim of the Peter Principle—tactics that worked in his lower-level political positions were not acceptable when escalated to the presidential level. But Nixon also succumbed to a deep-seated psychological need. His unchecked literary ambition involved him in creating bigger and bigger crises. Ultimately he became a victim of his own principle.

NIXON'S PRINCIPLE: If two wrongs don't make a right, try three.

TOO GOOD FOR THE JOB?

Most Americans remember Adlai Stevenson as a witty, eloquent, unsuccessful Democratic candidate for the presidency in 1952 and 1956, but he was much more. Born on February 5, 1900, he followed in the footsteps of his grandfather, Vice-President Adlai E. Stevenson, and devoted himself to public service. He served his country in many foreign relations posts and in 1961 was appointed ambassador to the United Nations.

One rumor states that Stevenson failed to win the presidency because he was too good for the job. Others claim he failed to win because he spoke over the heads of the people. It appears that everyone agrees that Stevenson talked over the heads of the people, but nobody admits to Stevenson's talking over his or her particular head. In an attempt to clarify this issue I am going to let Adlai speak for himself. Unfortunately he died on July 14, 1965, which was before I was able to conduct this interview, so his answers to my questions were selected from utterances he made during his lifetime.

PETER: The press says that the public doesn't trust you because you're too intelligent.

STEVENSON: Newspaper editors are men who separate the wheat from the chaff and then print the chaff.

PETER: Wasn't your approach too critical when compared to Eisenhower's paternalistic patriotism?

STEVENSON: Do not regard the critics as questionable patriots. What were Washington and Jefferson and Adams but profound critics of the colonial status quo?

PETER: But the critic may be very unpopular.

STEVENSON: A free society is one where it is safe to be unpopular.

PETER: It may be safe, but isn't an election a popularity contest?

STEVENSON: The idea that you can merchandise candidates for high office like breakfast cereal is the ultimate indignity to the democratic process. What we need, and find hard to get, is somebody who'll keep his hands out of other people's pockets.

PETER: Haven't the people been lied to so often they've lost faith?

STEVENSON: Those who corrupt the public mind are just as evil as those who steal from the public purse.

PETER: How do you feel about your two presidential campaigns?

STEVENSON: I suppose we have contrived few more exacting ordeals than a presidential campaign.

PETER: It is said that you lost because you talked over people's heads.

STEVENSON: Better to speak above people's heads than behind their backs.

PETER: What did you feel like when you lost?

STEVENSON: Oh, what I would really like is to just sit in the shade with a glass of wine in my hand and watch the dancers.

PETER: Didn't you attack those claiming to be liberal humanitarians but financial conservatives?

STEVENSON: I am not even sure what it means when one says he is a conservative in fiscal affairs and a liberal in human affairs. I assume what it means is that you will strongly recommend the building of a great many schools to accommodate the needs of our children, but not provide the money.

PETER: But didn't you give the Republicans a pretty bad time?

STEVENSON: I have been tempted to make a proposal to our Republican friends: that if they stop telling lies about us, we would stop telling the truth about them.

PETER: What's wrong with the GOP?

STEVENSON: The Republican Party was dragged kicking and screaming into the twentieth century.

PETER: Why did you direct most of your criticism at Richard M. Nixon?

STEVENSON: Nixon is the kind of politician who would cut down a redwood tree, then mount the stump for a speech on conservation.

PETER: What did you think of the public relations efforts to present him as the new Nixon?

STEVENSON: I don't wish to deprecate Nixon's new personality. But I do wish that we might hear some word from him repudiating the irresponsible, vindictive, and malicious words so often spoken by the impostor who has been using his name all these years.

PETER: What is the responsibility of government?

STEVENSON: The government must be the trustee for the little man, because no one else will be. The powerful can usually help themselves—and frequently do.

PETER: How are we doing in this regard?

STEVENSON: Since the beginning of time, governments have been mainly engaged in kicking people around. The astonishing achievement of modern times in the Western world is the idea that the citizens should do the kicking.

PETER: But doesn't that cause confusion?

STEVENSON: We believe it is better to discuss a question even without settling it than to settle a question without discussing it.

PETER: Is that your concept of government in a democracy?

STEVENSON: Government cannot be stronger or more tough-minded than its people. It cannot be more inflexibly committed to the task than they. It cannot be wiser than the people.

PETER: What is unique about American democracy?

STEVENSON: America is much more than a geographical fact. It is a political and moral fact—the first community in which men set out in principle to institutionalize freedom, responsible government, and human equality.

PETER: Now that you are ambassador to the United Nations how do you see America's place in international affairs?

STEVENSON: If total isolationism is no answer, total intervention is no answer either.

PETER: What is your hope for the UN?

STEVENSON: Just as Europe could never again be the old, closed-in community after the voyages of Columbus, we can never again be a squabbling band of nations before the awful majesty of space.

PETER: What do you consider the top priority of the United States?

STEVENSON: Our mission is the prevention, not just the survival, of a major war.

PETER: Are nuclear weapons our greatest threat?

STEVENSON: There is no evil in the atom; only in men's souls. I hope that we can make nuclear energy man's servant and not man's destructive master. Clearly this must be the test for which man's intelligence and the evolution of his thinking has been devised.

PETER: How can this be achieved?

STEVENSON: The journey of a thousand leagues begins with a single step. So we must never neglect any work of peace within our reach, however small.

PETER: We have run out of time. Do you have a final thought for my readers?

STEVENSON: Man does not live by words alone, despite the fact that sometimes he has to eat them.

WHEN IN DOUBT, MUMBLE

In the life of each great man there comes at least one challenge when he must pass the test of a "finest hour"—a time when man and circumstance contribute mutually to the establishment of the hero image.

Dr. James Harlan Boren's "hour" came on Tuesday, June 22, 1971, as he testified before the House Public Works Subcommittee on Investigation and Oversight (special congressional hearing on red tape).

After all other witnesses had trooped in to denounce the

escalation of government forms and reports and the avalanche of official paperwork (the federal government uses enough paper annually to construct a five-foot-wide ribbon of red tape around the earth and all the way to the moon), Dr. Boren appeared and offered this testimony of sweetness and light. He urged the committee not to get lost in a needless counting of forms or measuring of paper. He said, "Do we count the flakes of snow that give beauty and a sense of serenity to the countryside in winter? Do we count the drops of rain that nurture the trees and flowers that brighten our lives? Do we ration the canvas upon which the artist expresses his deepest feelings? Why then should we limit the paper with which the bureaucrat can create his special world?"

From the outset, it was clear that a new leader had bubbled to the surface of the political cesspool. As he proceeded to expound on "dynamic inaction and constructive non-responsiveness," he demonstrated his grasp of bureaucratic commitment to furthering the status quo by recommending a new Cabinet-level department of red tape. This department, to coordinate paperwork, would have divisions such as the Office of Overruns Permeations and Statistics (OOPS), Government Linguistics Obtusity Bureau (GLOB), Computerized Lethargic Output Division (CLOD), and Management Unit for Maximized Budgetary and Legal Evaluations (MUMBLE). Is it any wonder that this man, recommending to a congressional subcommittee more red tape, not less, was the president of the International Association of Professional Bureaucrats—bureaucratically abbreviated to INATAPROBU.

Jim Boren is the bureaucrat's bureaucrat—the incarnation of the only constant in the variable equation of the modern military-industrial-political complex. In every hierarchy in civilized society, bureaucrats, hiding among piles of paper, carbon copies, paper clips, punch cards, and computer printouts, have waited for the coming of a leader. The Boren genius lies in his sensitivity to the unmet needs of this immense unorganized segment of society, the professional bureaucrat. INATAPROBU is dedicated to optimizing the status quo by fostering adjustive adherence to procedural abstractions and rhetorical clearances by promoting feasibility studies, reviews, surveys of plans, surveys of feasibility studies, and surveys of reviews. Stated nonbureaucratically, dynamic inactivism is great input that produces little output.

Boren leaves his audiences laughing, but he also leaves them with a serious message. As president and founder (1968) of the International Association of Professional Bureaucrats he has been having a ball lampooning Washington bureaucrats, state bureaucrats, educational bureaucrats, any bureaucrats anywhere. He knows what bureaucrats are—he was one. He has been administrative assistant to former U.S. Senator Ralph Yarborough and deputy director of the U.S. Economic Mission to Peru. He holds a Ph.D. and has taught at high school and college levels.

Masquerading as the ultimate pompous bureaucrat, he tells his audiences that he stands ready to help make simple things more complex. He praises the accomplishments of

INATAPROBU's contributions to the prevention of mistakes by keeping things from happening and describes himself as a missionary in creative nonresponsiveness.

Boren is a genius at double-talk and employs this talent liberally during his many speaking engagements. His success on the lecture platform is also due to the fact that he looks and dresses like a cartoonist's version of the prototypical government officer. When he is not on lecture tours, he is writing books, taping radio shows, or conferring with card-carrying members of INATAPROBU.

Some of the bureaucratic principles INATAPROBU subscribes to are:

1. If you are going to be a phony, be sincere about it.
2. A top bureaucrat enjoys looking at the "big picture," for it is the overview that is important, and it is the overview that removes the administrator from the activity of the organization.
3. Bureaucrats are the only people in the world who can say absolutely nothing and mean it.
4. All mumblers are not bureaucrats—some are members of Congress or the House of Commons.
5. Bureaucratic leadership involves the jargon, not the message; the studies, not the conclusions; the procedure, not the results; and the image, not the reality.
6. A mumble can never be quoted.

Space does not permit a detailed account of Boren's and INATAPROBU's accomplishments, but here are just a few. Boren ran for President of the United States in 1972 as the Bureaucratic party's candidate. His promise "to make the world safe for bureaucracy" was widely endorsed.

To illustrate the deplorable conditions of our postal service, he put a saddlebag of mail on his horse in Philadelphia and deposited letters in the U.S. Mail at the same time. He rode his Pony Express to Washington, D.C., and delivered the mail three days before the U.S. Mail arrived.

At the Bureaucrats' Annual Award Banquet, Boren presents the "Order of the Bird" to bureaucrats who have achieved excellence in such bureaucratic arts as nitpicking, fuzzifying, and obfuscating. This award is a statue of an unfeathered, potbellied, sick bird.

To summarize his advice to bureaucrats everywhere, he presents:

BOREN'S GUIDELINES FOR BUREAUCRATS:
1. *When in charge, ponder.*
2. *When in trouble, delegate.*
3. *When in doubt, mumble.*

CHAPTER 6

Winning Isn't Everything

IN 1970, THE YEAR THAT *The Peter Principle* WAS PUBLISHED, Al Zavelle, general manager of Harvard Coop Bookstores, conceived a plan for conducting a poll based on the Peter Principle—in order to identify prominent persons who, in the opinions of the students, had risen to their levels of incompetence. He shared his idea with colleagues, and soon twenty-two university bookstores nationwide were involved in the balloting. The polls were open from February 14 to April 1, 1970. The question on the ballot was: "Who is the #1 famous person who best exemplifies The Peter Principle?"

TEN INCOMPETENTS OF 1970

1. Spiro Agnew
2. Richard Nixon
3. Claude Kirk
4. George Wallace
5. Lester Maddox
6. Lyndon Johnson
7. Ronald Reagan
8. John Lindsay

9. Julius Hoffman
10. Laurence Peter

I do not attempt to analyze these results beyond noting that at about the same time a Harris Poll was conducted to identify the Ten Most Admired Americans. This poll revealed that Richard Nixon was the winner with Spiro Agnew running a close second. The discrepancy between the Peter and Harris polls could be explained in a variety of ways. A statistician

FOR OUTSTANDING INCOMPETENCE

would explain that Nixon and Agnew were the most admired in one study and the most incompetent in another because the Harris Poll was based on a general population sampling and the Peter Principle Poll was based on the opinions of a select group of university students: those who frequented the book-stores. A sociologist would use the same evidence to prove the existence of the generation gap. A psychologist would explain Agnew's receiving 33.2 percent of the Peter Poll vote as a reaction to his derogatory comments about youths and intellectuals, while critics of the establishment would interpret the students' vote in relation to the subsequent fate of Nixon and Agnew as an example of the prophetic vision of youth and the Harris Poll as a basis for not trusting anyone over thirty.

In spite of the conflicting results, I am in favor of polls. The Motion Picture Academy Awards, the Ten Worst Dressed Women, the Best Sellers Lists, and the other opinion polls hold a certain fascination. Our curiosity makes us want to compare our opinions with those of the masses. It is the interpretation of the results of polls that leads to trouble. Eric Hoffer described this pathological aspect of interpretation when he said, "Our present addiction to pollsters and forecasters is a symptom of our chronic uncertainty about the future. Even when the forecasts prove wrong, we all go on asking for them. We watch our experts read the entrails of statistical tables and graphs the way the ancients watched their soothsayers read the entrails of a chicken."

THE GOLDEN DINOSAUR AWARDS

From the beginning of the "Peter's People" column for *Human Behavior,* the magazine has conducted a yearly Peter Principle Poll to determine the ten outstanding incompetents. The Peter Principle Golden Dinosaur Award was given in recognition of the winners. The dinosaur was chosen because it best symbolizes mindless escalation as a sure road to incompetence. Through increasing its size in an attempt to be number one, the dinosaur proved the inadvisability of gaining weight as a method of survival.

As a writer, in search of objective information, I am particularly interested in the results of each poll because it is the only authentic index of incompetency available today. Ira R. Manson, publisher of *Human Behavior,* in commenting on the poll said, "More than ever there seems to be a plethora of candidates. We no longer even pretend to reward and promote people solely on competence. Sometimes it seems that virtually every reason except competence—race, sex, national origin, religion and all those other things we were supposed to ignore before—is now used to place people in ever increasingly responsible positions."

In announcing the 1976 poll I encouraged the readers of *Human Behavior* to cast their votes and then, when the results were in, to rejoice in the fact that they had created a poll. This was to be a poll for polls' sakes—a poll conducted for the fun of conducting a poll.

An obvious limitation to the poll was that it identified only the already famous. Someone on your block could be a candidate for the Worst Dressed Woman list, but unless she was already a celebrity for some other reason, she would not be in the running. Your local service station could employ the world's worst mechanic, but his fame in your neighborhood would not earn him a place in the Incompetents' Hall of Fame.

The Peter Principle Poll
1976 Golden Dinosaur Award

1. Gerald Ford
2. Jimmy Carter
3. Richard Nixon
4. Earl Butz
5. Barbara Walters
5. Henry Kissinger
7. George Meany
8. Howard Cosell
9. Spiro Agnew
10. Robert Dole

The human animal differs from the lesser primates in his passion for lists of "Ten Best."

—H. ALLEN SMITH

Lists are so popular that *The Book of Lists*,[13] which is simply a book of lists, made the number one position on a list called the Best Sellers List.

My favorite lists are those derived from opinion polls because of their purity. Typically they are arrived at by surveying the opinions of a large number of individuals. The results are tabulated, and a list results. You may be delighted with it or infuriated by it, but you can't deny its existence.

The most popular slogan about winning is Vince Lombardi's "Winning isn't everything. It's the only thing." It is inconceivable that Jimmy Carter, who is number two on the 1977 Peter Principle Poll, is envious of Anita Bryant's number one position. Does the winner of the title "Worst Actor of the Year" agree that winning is everything?

The Peter Principle Poll
1977 Golden Dinosaur Awards

1. Anita Bryant
2. Jimmy Carter
3. Bert Lance
4. Howard Cosell
5. Andrew Young
6. Richard Nixon
7. Idi Amin
8. Laurence Peter
9. Barbara Walters
10. Billy Carter

In the spring of 1978 the government of British Columbia launched a campaign to promote tourism. The advertising centered on the two hundredth anniversary of Captain James Cook's landing on the west coast of Vancouver Island. While engaged in a quest for the elusive and imaginary Northwest Passage, Cook, in a dense fog, blundered into a bay with his two battered ships, the *Resolution* and the *Discovery*. The natives, Vancouver Island Nootka Indians, were so generous and helpful in making repairs to the ships that Cook named the area Friendly Cove. The bicentennial of Cook's arrival in

British Columbia seemed a suitable occasion for an official celebration for both tourists and British Columbians.

However, the descendants of the Nootka tribe who welcomed Cook and his men in 1778 were not at all enthusiastic about the festivities. The Indians' history of the event holds that Cook and his crew stole their food and possessions, ravished their women, and left the Nootka people infected with venereal disease as well as with a legacy of bitterness and lack of trust for white people.

The Indians responded to the government's bicentennial festivities by organizing a countercelebration. They attended official ceremonies and drowned out the speakers with drums and chants. They declared Friendly Cove to be unfriendly and off limits to visitors. They designed a T-shirt with a picture of a ship lost in the fog, with the words "COOK THE CAPTAIN" emblazoned across it.

The conflicting opinions on Cook are not unlike the extreme attitudes toward Anita Bryant, the first-place winner of the 1977 Peter Principle Poll. Anita Bryant topped another magazine poll when she was voted, by readers of *Good Housekeeping*, the number one most admired woman.

In another poll, teenage beauty contestants from across the nation voted Anita Bryant "America's greatest American." Sybil Shaffer of the Miss National Teen-Ager Contest announced in Atlanta that 3,500 girls who had entered their state pageants made Miss Bryant a landslide winner.

On the other hand, according to a poll published in the *Ladies' Home Journal*, high school students throughout the United States picked Anita Bryant and Adolf Hitler as the woman and man who have "done the most damage to the world." Anita Bryant was also matched with Richard Nixon as the top two who "made you angriest."

And then there was the question "If you could give a prize for achievement in religion, to which famous person would you give the prize?" Billy Graham came in first. God ran a close second. Anita Bryant, in spite of all her work on behalf of the Southern Baptists, didn't qualify for the "prize for achievement in religion." In another contest she even lost the race for office in the Southern Baptists Convention when she was defeated by a two to one majority in her bid for that denomination's first vice-presidency. All of which goes to prove that competence, like truth, beauty, and a contact lens, is in the eye of the beholder.

The Peter Principle Poll
1978 Golden Dinosaur Awards

1. Jimmy Carter
2. Anita Bryant
3. Andrew Young
4. Richard Nixon
5. Howard Jarvis
6. Howard Cosell
7. Idi Amin
   Phyllis Schlafly
8. John Briggs
9. Frank Rizzo
10. Ted Kennedy

For the first time there were eleven persons in the top ten because Phyllis Schlafly and Idi Amin tied for seventh place.

Jimmy Carter, who did well on previous Peter Principle Polls, placing second in 1976 and 1977, made it to the top in 1978. Considering that this was the first year that he had a full-time public relations person, Jerry Rafshoon, assigned to polishing his image, should not Rafshoon be recognized as the outstanding incompetent? Isn't incompetence clearly established when a person is assigned a specific task and the exact opposite is achieved? These questions are not intended as a criticism of the judgment of those who voted, but are asked that we may once again reflect on the criteria for judging competence. For whatever reasons we vote as we do, polls have become our modern means of expressing approval and disapproval and must therefore be regarded as the voice of the people.

CHAPTER 7

Ideas Whose Time Has Come

AN IDEA IN THE MIND OF AN INDIVIDUAL SCIENTIST COULD make a $100 billion defense system obsolete overnight. The mind of a single citizen somewhere in this world holds within it the potential of generating an idea that could lead us to the cure for cancer, the way to feed the starving millions, or the achievement of world peace.

The human brain is capable of conceiving an object as useful as a paper clip or a system as complicated as the space program. It is also capable of generating thoughts that bring us great joy or intense anxiety. In the following discussions of a few relatively simple concepts the focus is on ideas that are relevant to our everyday experience. "Voluntary Simplicity" presents ideas that may bring a new awareness of the available opportunities for a more rewarding life-style. "A Royal Flush" describes how a single invention made a significant contribution to human health and welfare as well as to our daily comfort. "The Government and Other Bulky Objects" provides fresh insights into the workings of our government. "The Power of Negative Thinking" reveals a dormant source of mental potential that you can release for use in solving many problems. In "Bureaucrats Beware" you will see that the

Washington red tape jungle and the high taxes you pay to support it can be brought under control, and in "What's Funny About That?" you will explore some of the ideas that make us laugh.

VOLUNTARY SIMPLICITY

As a child I was brought up in extreme poverty, but when I was old enough to get a job, I was able to upgrade my style of living progressively. Then in 1969, the success of the book *The Peter Principle* provided a new opportunity to raise my standard of living. I faced this opportunity with some misgivings. My wife, Irene, and I had seen some of our financially successful acquaintances increase their expenditures in such a way that they complicated their lives with more possessions than they needed, acquired more status and responsibility than they really wanted, and spent much of their time and energy maintaining and defending their newfound affluence. They had acquired possessions, and then it seemed that the possessions had acquired them.

We knew that we had hated the simplicity of the bare subsistence poverty had forced upon us in our early years. Being self-supporting wage earners had brought us many satisfactions. Now that we could afford more of the extras success had to offer, would we improve our lives or would we become caught up in acquiring more money, possessions, and status?

As we pondered this question, it became obvious that what we wanted was to improve the quality of our lives, not the quantity of things that symbolize success.

Financial independence had given us more control over some aspects of our lives. For example, I could now devote time to whatever projects I wished without consideration of the monetary outcomes. Irene and I could engage in hobbies and other recreational activities without primary concern for how much they would cost, and we could choose where we would live.

We decided that if we were going to bypass the materialistic corruption of our lives, we would have to avoid the fashionable preoccupation with money, status, and possessions. This required that we adopt a life-style of deliberate simplicity—one that was outwardly simple and inwardly rich.

Many have found simplicity in rural environments. Much as we admired the rugged individualism of those in the back-to-the-land movement, we were urban folk who wanted to be close to the city's great libraries, theaters, and cultural institutions. We wanted to be close to those things that would enrich our lives, and we wanted to be free of the complications that would prevent us from enjoying them. The small house, near the ocean, where we now live satisfied these requirements without demanding that we sacrifice too much time or effort on upkeep.

Our move toward deliberate simplicity was not an attempt to live cheaply, but an attempt to achieve a better balance between the material and nonmaterial components of life Each new acquisition, whether aesthetic or practical, was selected with careful consideration for its quality and permanence as well as for our real need. Our interest in beautiful objects, handcrafted of wood, stone, and natural fibers, led us to collect a few attractive things of lasting design. By seeking quality and permanence rather than quantity and stylishness, we live with things that bring enduring aesthetic satisfaction and a sense of security to daily living.

Until I replaced our cheap power lawn mower with the highest-quality hand mower obtainable, I would not have believed what a big step forward I was taking. The hand mower cost more but is a delight to operate. It never runs out of fuel. It never tests my patience getting started. It emits no pollutants. It provides me with healthful exercise. I can stop and start it with ease. I feel in control. I feel relieved of the nervous strain, the safety hazards, and the inevitable mechanical problems and responsibilities that power equipment entails. For us simplicity didn't come cheap, but the rewards were beyond price.

In evaluating the outcomes of the deliberate simplification of our material existence along with our attempts at enriching the intellectual, spiritual, emotional, and aesthetic qualities of life, we feel that we achieved a better balance between inner and outer growth. We had more time for ourselves. We invested more in love, fun, exploration, and healthful recreation. We spent more time in simple pleasures, walking on the beach, riding our bikes, and peaceful enjoyment of nature. Put simply, our deliberately simple life-style was our attempt to get more out of life for us. It worked. We struck a satisfying equilibrium that accommodated physical and material well-being with an improved psychological and spiritual life.

We have met others who have made similar discoveries, but we had no idea that the number of deliberate simplifiers was a significant social force. That is, not until I read an article by

Duane Elgin and Arnold Mitchell in the summer 1977 issue of *The CoEvolution Quarterly* [14] titled "Voluntary Simplicity (3)." ("Voluntary Simplicity (2)" was an earlier Stanford Research Institute paper by the same authors, and "Voluntary Simplicity (1)" was a 1936 article by Richard Gregg which was reprinted and included with the "Voluntary Simplicity (3)" *CoEvolution* article.) The authors describe the phenomenon of Voluntary Simplicity as a major social movement which has the potential of touching the United States and other developed nations to their cores. It could be the beginning of a major transformation of traditional American values, consumption patterns, institutional operations, social movements, and national politics. When the Stanford Research Institute found that the fastest-growing sector of the market is people who don't want to buy much, the business community took notice.

The authors emphasize the difficulty of making accurate predictions (the other kinds are easy to make) because Voluntary Simplicity is a social flow consisting of so many streams. It has its roots in the frugality and self-reliance of the Puritans, in Thoreau's vision at Walden Pond, in Emerson's plea for plain living and high thinking, and in the teachings of spiritual leaders such as Jesus and Gandhi. In recent years we have been witness to increased involvement in Eastern religions and philosophies, meditation, biofeedback, humanistic psychology, psychic phenomena, brain research into the rational and intuitive aspects of human nature, and other studies touching on the spiritual or nonmaterial dimensions of life. Consumerism stimulated many to be more discerning about quality and to purchase more durable products. Environmentalism has interested many in the disappearance of natural resources and contamination of the environment. These and other forces are behind the shift toward Voluntary Simplicity and range from the very personal concerns of those who, for purely selfish reasons like ours, find it a more rewarding life-style to those who see it as a solution to critical national problems.

Elgin and Mitchell report studies suggesting that 10 million American adults live by Voluntary Simplicity today. If many present conditions, such as chronic energy shortages and depletion of natural resources, along with the growing demands of the less developed nations for a more equitable share, the threat of environmental pollution by a throwaway society, disenchantment with the quality of products made for a mass market, a growing social malaise and purposelessness, and so on, continue to exist, it is predicted that by 1987 the numbers could exceed 40 million. By the year 2000 the number could be in excess of 90 million. This represents a phenomenal growth rate, but it would still be less than a third of the adult population by the beginning of the next century.

Although these figures are based on speculation about conditions existing in the future, they are worthy of consideration, thought, and discussion. Voluntary Simplicity may be critical to total individual fulfillment or even to human survival.

A ROYAL FLUSH

.I used to think that the epitome of fame was to become an entry in a dictionary. The Earl of Sandwich, in order not to leave the gaming table for meals, had his servant prepare him a snack consisting of a slice of meat between two pieces of bread. This not only allowed him to continue gambling but also resulted in the word "sandwich" becoming an entry in the reputable dictionaries of the English language. James Watt, who gave us the watt, Alessandro Volta, who gave us the volt, and James Parkinson, who gave us Parkinson's disease, are immortalized by appropriate dictionary entries.

Unfortunately certain names have more difficulty in gaining acceptance than others. On granting permission for Samuel Goldfish to become Samuel Goldwyn, Judge Learned Hand said, "A self-made man may prefer a self-made name."

What I am leading up to is the age-old question "What's in a name?" I agree with George Ade when he says, "There is everything in a name. A rose by any other name would smell as sweet, but would not cost half as much during winter months." Sticks and stones will break your bones, but your name can also be a liability.

Thomas Crapper [15] is an unsung hero whose contribution to human welfare and comfort is far greater than that of many of the scientists, physicians, statesmen, and patriots whose names we honor. Crapper invented the modern flush toilet.

Born in Yorkshire, England, in 1837, Thomas Crapper at the age of eleven walked to London to start work with a master plumber. (No child labor laws in those good old days.) By 1861, through hard work, ingenuity, perseverance, and foresight, Crapper was able to start his own business in Chelsea. It was here that he invented, tested, and built his flush toilet and gave to the world the convenience he called "Crapper's Valveless Water Waste Preventer."

The water closet, or WC, had been in use for many years, but it was a crude affair in which the flushing mechanism consisted of a large cistern from which the water was released through a pull-out-the-plug procedure. This wasted so much water that the London Board of Trade was fearful all the reservoirs would dry up. Thomas Crapper came to the rescue by inventing the modern flush tank, which dispensed enough water to flush the toilet and, after refilling of the tank, allowed the water to shut off automatically.

Crapper continued his experimental work and developed the modern venting system that prevented sewer gas from backing up into the rooms of the building. These two major contributions along with his many minor improvements make him truly the inventor of the modern toilet. Crapper was appointed Royal Plumber to Kings Edward VII and George V and installed beautifully embossed, flowered toilet bowls and tanks in Sandringham Palace.

Today at Sandringham, one of Queen Elizabeth II's huge private residences, after more than 100 years of faithful royal service, there still exist some authentic examples of Crapper's work. An original Crapper had an elegant bowl, topped with a seat of cedar because the wood was warm and subtly aromatic. Although a plumber to royalty, Crapper's invention has been a boon to mankind.

Thomas Crapper died in 1910, but it was not until American soldiers returned from World War I that his name gained widespread fame. It began by sayings such as "Going to the crapper" and "I need a crapper." By 1930 the *Dictionary of American Slang* reported that the term had come into common usage in America, but Webster's has no entry for "crapper," and the meaning given for "crap" is to lose in a game called craps. The raglan sleeve is named for Lord Raglan, the davenport is named for the Earl of Davenport, the cardigan is named for Lord Cardigan, but Crapper's contribution is still called a toilet.

CRAPPER'S LAW: A Royal Flush wins hands down.

THE GOVERNMENT AND OTHER BULKY OBJECTS

Most Americans have learned to tolerate, if not relish, the inefficiencies of their giant bureaucracies. Some individuals show more concern and try to understand the escalating nature of the institutional control over their lives. The aware citizen, living from crisis to crisis—national emergencies, energy and food shortages, inflation, corruption within the FBI and CIA, rip-offs, and breakdown of the processes of government—cannot but be apprehensive concerning the non-responsiveness of the modern military-industrial-political complex. Furthermore, the sagas of the failures and finagling of major public and private institutions, Lockheed, the Pentagon, welfare, education, and law enforcement are all examples of bureaucratic ineptitude, wherein escalation of expenditure reaches colossal proportions while real achievement is minimal.

A congressional subcommittee conducted a study and issued a report saying federal government paperwork costs $8 billion a year. At the rate of one per second, it would take 2,000 years to destroy all government records, the committee said. The subcommittee also noted that $100 to $200 million could be saved by writing shorter, more concise letters. The subcommittee's report was seventy pages long on the bureaucratic theory that brevity is the soul of witlessness.

Paul Tabori, in his book *The Natural Science of Stupidity*,[16] included this example: "When promising U.S. soldiers were sent to colleges for engineering courses during World War II, the assignments were made alphabetically. Of 300 soldiers arriving at one small Southern school, 298 were named Brown."

In answer to a request for information on the guaranteed annual wage, the Bureau of Labor Statistics included a pamphlet entitled *The 1955 Ford and General Motors Union Contracts*. The item was listed as "Unnumbered Reprint #116."

Robert N. Kharasch provides rational explanations why so many work so long and so hard to produce so little. Efficiency and achievement, he believes, are entirely secondary to the existence of the institution because it is activity for activity's sake, not the result, that matters.

In his book *The Institutional Imperative; How to Understand the United States Government and Other Bulky Objects*,[17] Kharasch presents a dazzling array of laws, principles, and axioms, describing how the *function* of an agency is seen as its *purpose*. The development of the C-5A aircraft provides an illustration. The C-5A was originally conceived by the Pentagon as a monstrous cargo plane with 1,700 square feet of usable level floor space and the capacity to airlift a weight of more than 200 tons. The inevitable committee or planning group was assembled. The Lockheed Aircraft Corporation contracted to build the planes at $28 million each. The planning group then established liaison with a vast number of departments within the military complex. The plane-planning group coordinated all the accumulated data and integrated everybody's ideas into the plans for the C-5A. The original monster became a lumbering mammoth that included the additional specifications for meeting the participants' demands. The additional weight resulted in the need for increase in takeoff and landing capabilities, so specifications and costs spiraled upward. The outcome was a $29 million overrun per plane.

This example was made available through the auspices of Ernest Fitzgerald, an Air Force auditing officer, who became aware that expenses were far outrunning estimates. He began asking questions. The Air Force was not amused. The last thing it wanted was an inside expert exposing the obvious fact that the institution was manned by comparative simpletons. Fitzgerald was transferred to an inert position and then chucked out. The Air Force's explanation for firing Fitzgerald was a perfect example of bureaucratic irony. The reason given was "to save expenses." The final resolution appeared to be institutionally satisfactory. The Air Force ended up with big fat monstrous planes costing more than double the original contract price, and the Lockheed Aircraft Corporation was saved again by transfusions of large sums of public monies.

KHARASCH'S AXIOM: Whatever the internal machinery does is perceived within the institution as the real purpose of the institution.

THE POWER OF NEGATIVE THINKING

When I hear Norman Vincent Pealing,
I get that awful run-down feeling.

Like most of my contemporaries, I was indoctrinated with the popular philosophy called positive thinking. Trying to live by this approach, I experienced the most unhappy and frus-

trating years of my life. Yet through it all I struggled to keep alive the wishful-thinking optimism of a true believer. I set goals for myself that I could not achieve, believing that happiness and success were a matter of keeping my vibes jangling in concert with the cosmos. My positive expectations led to frequent disappointments and unfulfilled wishes, because I did not realize that the yellow brick road led only to more yellow bricks.

The day eventually arrived when I gave up this optimistic, opinionated, positive nonsense, opting for the realities of achievement in lieu of the better days that never seem to come. I began appreciating the good things that were happening to and around me. Life was no longer a struggle for unobtainable goals. I had, at long last, discovered the *Power of Negative Thinking*.

You can imagine my delight, after ten joy-filled years of living by this new negative philosophy, when I came across a newly published slim volume called *How to Cure Yourself of Positive Thinking* (subtitled *The Book That Bares the Fallacies, Traps, and Tragic False Hopes of Positive Thinking—and Makes a Brilliant Case for Putting New Order, Joy, and*

Freedom in Your Life by Being Negative).[18] As I made my way through the book, I was repeatedly treated to that most rewarding experience: reading the words of an author who had made the same discoveries about how to live that I had.

So I interviewed Donald G. Smith, the author, who turned out to be the kind of easygoing, mild-mannered, happy, practical philosopher the book had led me to expect.

Here is my attempt at a summary of his arguments in favor of negative thinking. His main point is that as seekers of truth in a world constantly being pushed, pulled, and tugged by Madison Avenue and becoming weary of change just for the sake of change, we should learn to say NO to the fatuous homilies currently masquerading as truth. As each of us struggles to make a successful journey through this life, we should be guided by the realities of existence. If we are to thrive and prosper, we must learn to live in a world of *what is* and *what can be*.

The problem with the philosophy of positive thinking is that it is based on wishing-on-a-star nonreality. When put into words, it becomes a verbal weapon used to clobber anyone with the effrontery to disagree. "Stop being so negative," has become the ultimate put-down hurled at anyone with the good sense to see through the wrongness of a proposed monumental absurdity. It is, in fact, a club—masquerading as an eternal verity—used to keep an upstart in his place and to grease the way for the progress of colossal absurdities. But unless we cure ourselves of positive thinking and acquire the strength to say No to the inefficiency, delusions, misinformation, and tragic false hopes of the myth peddlers, we will be doomed to frustrating lives spent anticipating a better day lurking around the next bend in the road. The most dangerous aspect of positive thinking is that it carries its own no-fail feature. If it doesn't work, you just weren't trying hard enough.

One of the most mystifying aspects of positive thinking is

that people who receive the least in rewards seem to believe with the most intensity. They are convinced that it works when obviously it doesn't work at all. They believe that if they concentrate on some great benefit to themselves, some sort of force will be put into play that will align the energies of the universe with the realization of their objectives.

The reason that positive thinkers fail is that their philosophical processes start with a false premise. They believe that goodness is something to be achieved and, therefore, that one must devise some means of achieving it.

Negative thinking presupposes that goodness is nothing more than the absence of badness and that life, the world, the energies already flowing around us are essentially good. Without disruption there is harmony; without noise there is quietness; without disagreement there is agreement; without drunkenness there is sobriety; without sickness there is health; without impedance there is flow. Without unhappiness, discord, failure, and frustration we can look forward to happy, fruitful, and productive lives. In that happiness is not a commodity, we do not therefore require the services of a mystic to help us find it, nor do we need to wait for Aries to descend into the fifth house of Scorpio on the third Thursday of the month. Not true, says Smith. These are the disillusioned positives who found out that it doesn't work and haven't the foggiest notion what to do about it.

Unfortunately positive thinkers have created a stereotype of the negative thinker as a lonely, sour individual standing in the way of technological progress. It is not surprising that positive thinkers have the gall to take credit for human progress when, in fact, invention is part of an evolutionary process in the inevitable expansion of knowledge. Thus, the telegraph naturally followed the comprehension of electricity, followed in turn by the telephone, radio, radar, and television. It is a normal progression. Positive thinking doesn't make it happen, and negative thinking doesn't prevent it from happening.

When we read the inspiring story of Charles Lindbergh, for example, we are told of his strong will and determination. Without in anyway minimizing the greatness of his feat, Smith points out that Lindbergh was a top airmail pilot and was as thoroughly qualified to attempt the Atlantic crossing as any man alive. Although the risks were great, he set a reasonable goal. In 1927 a competent pilot in the right airplane could fly the Atlantic alone. Under any other conditions it couldn't be done, and all the positive thinking in the world couldn't have got him from New York to Paris. Lindbergh, according to Donald Smith, wasn't a positive thinker. He was a realist, as Edison, Watt, Columbus, and Marco Polo were realists—hard-nosed, practical men who went forward and attained the attainable.

One of Smith's major complaints, perhaps the prime force in his NO campaign, is the number of totally unqualified people making important and binding decisions. Thus, the travel route is planned by someone who can't read a map; the publication schedule is set by the person who knows the least about book production and marketing; the athletic budget is established by an official who knows nothing about sports; personnel policies and decisions can be expected to originate with a social misfit who has had a lifetime problem getting along with people; the protest march is led by a loudmouth who has little or no comprehension of the issue at hand. No matter what the endeavor, Smith says, we can be assured that a total ignoramus will emerge from the pack and present himself as a latter-day Moses, leading us, unfortunately, back into Egypt.

The need, therefore, is for people with courage and good sense to stand up and say NO!

SMITH'S MAXIM: In most group undertakings, the final decision will be made by the person who is the least qualified to make it.

BUREAUCRATS BEWARE

Sid Taylor is a short man with a towering idea. His idea is called System Simplification (SYSIM). What kind of man would devote his life to simplifying systems in a world bent on making things more complex? I was astonished to find that for twenty years he had been a systems expert for the Pentagon, that bastion of meaningless paperwork. Before his tour of duty with the Pentagon he had been a World War II bomber command officer.

Since his retirement from the Pentagon he has become the research director for the National Taxpayers Union. In this new role he has led a crusade against federal waste and deficit budgeting.

Taylor is a dynamic man who hasn't lost his military bearing now that he is in civilian life. He is a prolific writer who issues a barrage of letters and press releases on behalf of National Taxpayers Union causes and in his spare time lectures on System Simplification to many interested groups. I interviewed him in his office-apartment in Arlington, Virginia. He prefers to live and work in this simplified environment rather than to travel to work at the NTU offices located in a Capitol Hill office building.

PETER: How does it feel to be the voice of simplicity and economy in Washington?

TAYLOR: I feel like the world is a tuxedo and I'm a pair of brown shoes.

PETER: I have a special reason for interviewing you at this time. President Carter has promised to reduce the amount of bureaucratic paperwork. What success do you expect he will have?

TAYLOR: President Carter is an admirer of efficiency. However, he faces an almost impossible job. Our income tax system, for example, with a six-thousand-page tax code, is a *Catch-22* red tape nightmare. Welfare and food stamps systems leak billions of tax dollars each year to the wrong people. We're supporting both the needy and the greedy. Our federal housing program has misspent billions to make Uncle Sam the nation's biggest slumlord. Our mass transit program has spent a billion dollars reinventing the electric trolley car. To avoid embarrassment, the bureaucrats now call it a people mover. Our Social Security system has become a four-trillion-dollar actuarial deficit disaster. The U.S. Postal Service requires a one-billion-dollar-a-year taxpayer subsidy. Do you know that the federal government now operates more than ninety systems in the billion-dollar taxpayer cost category. The President's success in reducing paperwork will depend in large measure on his success in improving many aspects of government bureaucracies.

PETER: How can he achieve this?

TAYLOR: Through System Simplification.

PETER: But isn't government bureaucracy highly resistant to improvement?

TAYLOR: Naturally one cannot expect the watchdog to bite himself.

PETER: Have you formulated a law of simplicity?

TAYLOR: *THE LAW OF SIMPLICITY: Fat systems die young.*

PETER: Would you explain?

TAYLOR: Systems are subject to the Law of Simplicity—a cradle-to-grave cycle of growth to decay. A new system is born as a relatively simple, inexpensive, and effective solution. It often replaces an older, more complex, costly, and time-consuming way of doing the job. However, as the new system ages, it expands while deteriorating in three stages: one, red tape (delays); two, red lights (defects); three, red ink (deficits).

PETER: Why does it expand?

TAYLOR: The system tends to become the victim of its own overhead, paperwork, rules enlargement, program changes, malfunctions, overorganization, et cetera. When it reaches stage three, it begins to collapse under its own delays, defects, and deficits. At this point it may be replaced by a newer and simpler idea.

PETER: But aren't there exceptions?

TAYLOR: Yes, the government has some systems that are supported for years regardless of the costs. And the government supports inefficiency in the so-called private sector, as in the case of Lockheed.

PETER: Are there other causes beyond those of internal decay?

TAYLOR: Yes, an external threat may exist in the form of new technology, new competition, or changes in legislation. An entire system can be made obsolete almost overnight by a new scientific discovery, a change in the competitive environment, a new invention, or a new law.

PETER: Is there a difference between internal and external causes in terms of outcomes?

TAYLOR: Whether the system reaches the red ink stage because of internal or external causes, it literally has one foot in the funeral parlor. It's merely a matter of time before technology or innovation invents a better mousetrap. Necessity is the mother of invention, and Simplicity is the father. When these two get together, a better system is born. It's happening every day in every profession, business, industry, and even sometimes government.

PETER: What can be done to prevent system deterioration and bureaucratic expansion?

TAYLOR: First we must understand what is happening to the system. The trick is to recognize the difference between red tape and meaningful records and to see the red lights before the system, business, or product approaches stage three (red ink).

PETER: Then your System Simplification still relies on human judgment or wisdom?

TAYLOR: Right! Efficiency requires judgment, as does the selection of what we are trying to be efficient about. It is better to be ten percent efficient in achieving something worthwhile than to be a hundred percent efficient in achieving something worthless.

PETER: Is there sufficient wisdom to meet today's needs?

TAYLOR: That is difficult to say. Wisdom is such a fleeting phenomenon.

PETER: Will you explain?

TAYLOR: One of the tragedies of mankind is that wisdom is perishable. Unlike information or knowledge, it cannot be stored in a computer or recorded in a book. It expires with each passing generation. For the most part, man does not learn from history. He repeats history often at great cost and bloodshed. In the learning curve of life, he is generally too busy coping with present events to benefit from the past. Each new generation generates its own mistakes and stupidity. From a wisdom-based, decision-making viewpoint, civilization is only about seventy years old. In terms of accumulated wisdom it is no older or wiser than the living senior citizens of the current generation. Wisdom does not accumulate over the ages like knowledge or technology. It is acquired briefly, in varying degrees, and often too late by each current generation. Each generation has to go through the learning curve of wisdom in its own short life-span. Wisdom is a rare and transient commodity that cannot be inherited, sold, or given away. Producing wisdom and better value judgments in today's fast-moving, thermonuclear, technology-laden, space-age environment may prove to be mankind's most urgent challenge. In this context, it is important to recognize that the computer is not a wisdom machine.

PETER: Now you are picking on the computer.

TAYLOR: The computer is a great invention. Unfortunately it has some undesirable side effects in changing the way we think, reason, and make decisions. The peril of the digital computer lies in its mindless, machine logic. Its binary circuitry can think only digital or numeric. However, the big problems facing humankind today involve value judgments or analog logic, and this is outside the realm of computer competence.

PETER: Your twenty years as a systems expert have not blunted your analog logic.

TAYLOR'S LAW: There is no such thing as government money—there is only taxpayers' money.

WHAT'S FUNNY ABOUT THAT?

What is ethnic humor? What is Jewish humor? What is black humor? What is Italian humor? What do they have in

common? The usual answer, although not necessarily the correct answer, is that ethnic humor grew out of one tragedy or another. Jewish humor was a response to religious persecution. Black humor was a reaction to the plight of people in slavery. It is reasonable to assume that an oppressed people, without the power to improve their lot, would laugh at themselves and joke about their situation. When people laugh at themselves and their situation, no matter how distressing that situation may be, emotionally they rise above the degradation of their situation. An oppressed people able to laugh at its oppression appears to be superior to its oppressors.

Prejudice, oppression, and bigotry are ugly aspects of the human condition. Offensive acts are not funny, but when the victims of cruelty respond with humor, they ease their own suffering temporarily. The subtlety of this conflict between tragic situations and humorous responses is the basis of much that has become entertainment. Even the symbols of the theater are the masks of comedy and tragedy. Tears and laughter, which seem to be at opposite poles, are in reality closely related.

There is another type of ethnic humor that is based not on oppression but on real or imagined racial or ethnic characteristics. The frugality of the Scots is the basis of thousands of Scottish jokes. Many of the best are told by Scots about themselves. I read a letter to the editor written by a Scot who complained bitterly about the newspaper's jokes about tight-fisted Scotsmen. He ended the letter with threats of discontinuing borrowing and reading his neighbor's paper. There are jokes about the combative Irish, the boastful American, the humorless Englishman, the stupid Pole, and the cunning Japanese that are not based on ghetto life or other overt oppression. This form of ethnic humor is at its best when presented by a member of the ethnic group that is the subject of the humor.

I wouldn't go so far as the great Bulgarian humorist Iliya Beshkov when he said, "A nation which has not created its own humor has not secured its right to existence," but I do feel that any nation or group of people whose members cannot see humor in being of that nationality or group is immature.

One ethnic group that has made a fine art of laughing at itself consists of the residents of Gabrovo, Bulgaria. The Gabrovonian enjoys making others laugh, so he makes up anecdotes at his own expense. Originally the town of Gabrovo became known for its knives and other metal products, as well as for its wooden utensils and homespun woolen cloth. Gabrovonian merchants traveled the Ottoman Empire to sell the products of the Gabrovonian craftsmen.

The profit margin was small, so the Gabrovonians developed a respect for their earnings and practiced extreme economy. A folklore of anecdotes about exceptional thrift, which originally was based on reality, persisted as the Gabrovo economy grew. The tradition survives, and the Gabrovonian spins yarns of his poverty-stricken existence when he is no longer poor or even when he possesses great wealth. The comic element of the Gabrovo anecdote is its many variations on a single theme—the Gabrovonian proverbial thrift. Gabrovonians cut off their cats' tails to save heat in winter when doors are opened to let the animals in or out. They stop their clocks at night to save wear and tear on the gears. They bury their dead upright to save space.

When asked about his wedding ring, a Gabrovonian replied, "My wife is wearing it this week."

A father bought his son a new pair of shoes and then instructed him to take bigger strides.

Gabrovonians put green-tinted glasses on their horses and feed them shavings which the horses think is hay.

They give their honored guests homing pigeons as tokens of devotion and trust.

Gabrovonian men choose slim women for wives, knowing that they will use less calico for a dress.

When they make a purchase, they want it wrapped in today's paper.

A Gabrovonian invitation read: "Come and see me in Gabrovo, and I'll take you to see our neighbors, to give you an idea of how they welcome people."

Gabrovonians claim they invented narrow trousers, short skirts, and matchboxes with only one side for striking.

Having no experience with Bulgarians and knowing little about Gabrovonians, I find their humor most appealing. My impression is of a fun-loving people who want to share their ethnic jokes. If I were strongly prejudiced against Bulgarians, I might repeat these stories as a reflection of my hostility to support a stereotype of Gabrovonians as miserly tightwads. So it seems that humor about any racial, national, religious, or social group can be either ethnic or anti-ethnic, depending on who is telling the joke and on the motivation.

The question of whether a joke is in good taste seems to be more a matter of degree than of subject matter. If one wants to talk about human dignity or say that certain subjects should not be joked about, then all jokes are in bad taste because the purpose of humor is to prick the bubble of pomposity and to make light of subjects that may be taken too seriously.

If all humor is in bad taste, and I believe that it is, why are ethnic jokes acceptable in one period and not in another? Revolutionaries can't afford to be funny. They are only as strong as their prejudices, and seeing humor in their own prejudices is the one sure way to weaken them. Even as benign a revolution as the Women's Liberation Movement is hostile to humor. Jewish humor, in which Jews perceive and express the irony of Jewish life, has been prolific through the ages but was suppressed during the current revolutionary period of heightened Jewish consciousness. Black humor by black people about life as a black person is now emerging as a rich and varied ethnic humor following a period of put-down-of-whitey jokes that paralleled the most dynamic period of the black rights movement. And so it seems that groups, like individuals, have periods of hypersensitivity in which their sense of humor is impaired by identity problems, revolutionary zeal, or other needs for compulsive seriousness. These periods of hypersensitivity pass as the problems that created them are resolved. John F. Kennedy used to say, "There are three things which are real: God, human folly, and laughter. The first two are beyond our comprehension. So we must do what we can with the third."

Fortunately for me, I feel no personal involvement in the problems of ethnicity. I am a Canadian—a nonpersecuted minority with no identity problems or, to put it another way, no identity. I expend so much effort explaining to Americans that I am not English and so much effort explaining to the English that I am not American that I have no energy left to be Canadian. I am actually a true cosmopolitan—I can be miserable anywhere. Canadians and Americans are a lot alike in that we share a common language—broken English.

Let me cite an example of the Canadian thought process. In 1913 the Canadian Manufacturers Association held a convention in Toronto. The main item on the agenda was the adoption of a slogan to promote the sale of Canadian goods to Canadians. After three days of deliberation they selected a motto that was so good that it is used to this day. The slogan is "Made in Canada."

Today there are 23 million Canadians divided into three language groups. Those that speak French are called Quebecers. Those that speak English are called Anglos. Those that speak both French and English are called show-offs.

The goal of every young ambitious Canadian is to grow up and join the civil service and qualify for a government pension.

A Canadian swimming pool is something you shouldn't walk on because the ice may be thinner than it looks.

A waitress asked me a riddle. "What's the difference between a Canadian and a canoe?" "A Canadian doesn't tip."

A Canadian thinks he's a conservationist if he uses a Kleenex for a second blow.

An old saying goes, "Laugh and the world laughs with you. Frown and they'll think you're Canadian."

Two members of the Canadian Liberal party met. The first said, "I didn't see you at the last meeting of the Liberal party." The second said, "If I'd known it was the last meeting, I'd have brought the whole family."

You can tell if a Canadian is still alive by feeling his nose to see if it is still running.

And finally, these comments about Canada:

Americans are benevolently ignorant about Canada, while Canadians are malevolently well informed about the United States.

—J. BARTLET BREBNER

When they said Canada, I thought it would be up in the mountains somewhere.

—MARILYN MONROE

I don't even know what street Canada is on.

—AL CAPONE

CHAPTER 8

There Ought to Be a Law

OUR LAWBOOKS ARE CLUTTERED WITH STATUTES THAT HAVE become obsolete, along with cockeyed ordinances that never did make much sense. Fortunately most of the time we don't let these completely smother our country's sound and workable regulations, but the fact remains that on the legal front we have far too many laws.

There are various nonlegal laws that provide nothing but help and solace, and these are the aphoristic laws of human and institutional behavior. Not only do they provide a rationale for our foibles, but even more important, they sometimes help us laugh at ourselves. These laws contribute to our understanding of corporate and government bureaucracy and explain why we live in a bungleland of mishaps, delays, blunders, confusion, and induced group hysteria or even paranoia. It is my opinion that we will never have too many of these laws.

Murphy's and Parkinson's Laws and the Peter Principle are the best-known contributions to this area of social science, but contemporary bureaucracies and our response to them constitute too rich a vein of human foible to yield completely to just three formulations. In this chapter I have assembled in one place what I consider to be the best of these laws and theories explaining the intentional or unintentional malice, mischief, and incompetence with which we all struggle to cope.

In some cases a deceptively simple law expresses a profound truth about human affairs:

HARDIN'S LAW: You can never do merely one thing.

This formulation by University of California, Santa Barbara, biologist Garrett Hardin applies to any action that changes something in a complex system, such as the natural environment or human society. Even when an action is successful in achieving its intended result, it also has outcomes that were not intended, and these may offset or outweigh that intended result. Hardin's Law, with its illuminating quality, is not presented as an excuse for inertia, but it does call for us to try to be tough-minded and to think in more complex terms.

Another example of a casual-sounding law worthy of serious thought is:

PETRIE'S LAW: When you're starting an organization, twelve people are one too many.

Jesus Christ was the first to discover this principle, but his crucifixion interfered with his formulating it as a law. The principle was rediscovered many years later by employers who observed that fewer people who are paid more tend to produce excellence at no overall increase in cost.

It is a common experience to be pleased and satisfied when one reads something that is clear and precise, but when one reads this message from the U.S. Office of Environmental Education: "The prioritization of developmental activities concerned with the identification, conceptualization and characterization of the content and structure of effective, responsive activities vis-à-vis the Environmental Education Act's definition of environmental education over general dissemination and evaluation activities arose from the widespread confusion about environmental education," one is more likely to be dissatisfied and engage in further discussion and further discussion and further discussion.

CAMUS'S LAW: Those who write clearly have readers; those who write obscurely have commentators.

There are many other originators of statements who failed to grasp the importance of their own words and neglected to label them as laws. I have long had a preoccupation with the concisely and cleverly worded phrase that makes a pointed observation. Today, frustrated by proliferating political and bureaucratic verbiage, I find myself searching for brief, straightforward pronouncements that actually say something worthwhile. When I discover a particularly witty example, I like to honor it by providing it with a title. For example, when Yogi Berra said, "You can observe a lot just by watching," I named it Berra's Axiom. In identifying these gems and in providing appropriate labels, I hope to help preserve them for future generations.

The late Richard J. Daley, mayor of Chicago, was ridiculed by the pundits of the press for his misuse of language. Although his grammar and choice of words often failed to comply with the rules of formal English, I found his declarations to be models of clarity. One of his pronouncements involved such a brilliant choice of words that I decided to award it one of my special labels.

DALEY'S LAW: We will reach greater and greater platitudes of achievement.

Although the thoughtful reader will immediately recognize the validity of this deceptively simple sounding law, I would like to defend it with a few examples that demonstrate its universality.

POLITICS. A disgusted member of the Australian Parliament described a session of the Australian legislature: "Nine members were present out of one hundred and twenty-four; of these, three were sleeping, two were solving cross-word puzzles, and one was reading a Donald Duck comic book."

And here in America one of the developments on the national scene has been the political nonjob. A major part of old-fashioned political patronage consisted of providing employment for the party faithful. Unfortunately this provided little incentive or reward for the well-heeled and well-placed political supporter. The political nonjob was created to provide the wealthy, loyal party member with the satisfaction of appointment to a high-sounding presidential commission and with an impressive presidential document with which to adorn his office wall.

Harry Dent, a presidential political aide, made promises to the Republican National Committee that it would have a strong voice in the awarding of nonjob patronage. Apparently nobody knows for sure how many "nonsubstantive" posts have been created, but during the Nixon era it was estimated that the membership was somewhere between 8,000 and 10,000. Some governmental commissions that were created to advise Congress and the executive branch had no meetings, no offices, no staff, and issued no reports.

A classic example of how one department of government actually works to defeat another occurred in Canada. The Department of Regional Expansion solicited American industry to invest in Canada and offered a bonus of $30,000 for each job created by companies establishing new plants or expanding old plants in Canada. At the same time the Canadian minister of finance proposed setting up the Canadian Development Corporation to "buy back" American industry located in Canada.

And in the field of political noncommunication few could beat Canadian External Affairs Minister Paul Martin's response to a question by the Toronto press, regarding external aid: "Don't quote me as saying that we will or we should increase our external aid. That would be my opinion if I had an opinion, but as a member of my government, I don't have an opinion."

LAW. A recent news release carried the following information: "The Washington State House of Representatives is considering the legalization of prostitution, providing [sic] the women are of good character."

MILITARY. During World War II it was found necessary to revise the manual for operation of fifteen-pound guns. An officer was puzzled, during the showing of a training film, by the fact that Gunner No. 6 stood smartly at attention throughout the entire film. An inquisitive officer made lengthy inquiries about the duties of Gunner No. 6. Eventually he found a veteran of the Boer War who explained that Gunner No. 6 held the horses while they fired the cannon.

PUBLIC HEALTH. *The American Journal of Public Health* carried the following explanation: "One on the outside who criticizes the placement of square pegs in round holes should be sure that there are not more round holes and square pegs than there are square holes and round pegs. Even if this is not the case the critic should be certain that round holes are not a more serious problem than square ones, and he should withhold his criticism unless he is quite sure that it is better to leave round holes unfilled than it is to fill them partially with square pegs."

H. Allen Smith made a significant contribution to the law field by clarifying the difference between Gumperson's Law and Fetridge's Law.

GUMPERSON'S LAW: The contradictory of a welcome probability will assert itself whenever such an eventuality is likely to be most frustrating, or, in other words, the outcome of a given desired probability will be inverse to the degree of desirability.

Smith simplified *GUMPERSON'S LAW* to read: *Vacant parking spaces are always on the other side of the street.* Example: You can plant grass seed in rich, fertilized, and well-watered soil and it will not grow, although the few seeds that settle into a crack in the blacktop driveway take root and flourish. Example: When your car is functioning perfectly, there is a service station on every corner, but when the engine starts to malfunction, the stations are miles apart. Example: Plumbing always stops functioning on Saturday night.

FETRIDGE'S LAW: Important things that are supposed to happen do not happen, especially when people are looking.

Example: Your talking myna bird has learned an impressive repertoire of cute sayings, but when your friends are summoned to hear him, he clams up. Example: Your television set is flickering. The repairman can find nothing wrong. In his presence it works perfectly. After he leaves, you settle down to your favorite program, and the picture resumes flopping.

Fetridge's Law operates violently in the realms of medicine and dentistry. Fierce pain requiring immediate attention often stops as you move from the waiting room to the doctor's office. As Smith points out, although Fetridge's Law can be exasperating, it has its goods points. It can cure toothache.

In 1971 I was writing about a man who was successful in business because he was aware of the need for his services. The story needed a punch line to emphasize the importance of being "plugged in" to opportunity, but I couldn't get the wording that seemed right. That evening, while reading the paper, I saw one of those short fillers at the end of a column:

SATTINGER'S LAW: It works better if you plug it in.

There was the closing line I was looking for. In a few words it expressed what I wanted to say about the importance of being aware, tuned-in, or in contact with opportunity. Two years later I received the following letter:

Dear Dr. Peter,

I note that Sattinger's Law is quoted in your recent book *The Peter Prescription*. You may be interested to know that Sattinger's Law was originally promulgated as a defense against Mrs. Sattinger's Law:

MRS. SATTINGER'S LAW: If it doesn't work, we need a new one.

Sincerely yours,
IRVIN J. SATTINGER

So far in this book 38 laws have been cited. The next three topics, "Murphy's Laws," "Parkinson's Laws," and "Peter's Principles," include 73 entries. The final section, "Other Laws from A to Z," contains 387 items not referred to as laws in the previous chapters. These laws are presented without examples, proof, or research as each will be self-evident to the thoughtful reader.

I have generally avoided laws that apply to unusual professions and unique situations. Far from being the last word on the subject, this selection of 498 laws, corollaries, etc., just scratches the surface of a great source of wit and wisdom. My recommendation to the interested reader is that you start your own collection of laws that apply to your profession, your life, and your special interests.

MURPHY'S LAWS

Recently I read a scientific paper about earthquakes called "If You Build Your House on a Crack in the Earth, It's Your Own Fault." In spite of the double meaning in that title, it

does express an important principle: If you do stupid things, you will reap abysmal results. But there is another large class of happenings that do not adhere to this rule. You put your car through the car wash, and within three hours it starts to rain. You buy an umbrella, and the rain stops. You get in the tub for a nice warm bath, and the doorbell rings. You sit on the toilet, and at the most critical moment the phone rings. In these instances you can do everything right, and still, the results are wrong. This category of events was clearly enunciated in:

> *MURPHY'S LAW: If anything can go wrong, it will go wrong.*

Murphy's Law caught on and was quoted everywhere as the explanation for blunders and accidents. Of all the published responses to Murphy's original dictum only one offered any criticism:

> *THE REALISTS' COMMENT ON MURPHY'S LAW: Murphy is an optimist.*

Soon after his first law appeared in print, about thirty years ago, there started a stream of interdisciplinary and specialized tenets credited to Murphy. His original edict was renamed Murphy's First Law by those wishing to distinguish it from those that followed. After a few years, I was forced to develop my own classification system in order to continue my research. This was necessary because the various lists contained numerous redundancies, and each list had a different numbering system. Many of the laws were subsets of his original observation and provided insight to specific situations and professions. All these new laws tended to verify the validity of his first principle. The first law and those that follow constitute the Peter Taxonomy of Murphy's Major Laws. It does not include those attributed to Murphy that were inconsistent with his original viewpoint and were obviously the work of impostors.

MURPHY'S SECOND LAW: Nothing is as easy as it looks.

MURPHY'S THIRD LAW: Everything takes longer than you think.

MURPHY'S FOURTH LAW: Left to themselves, things tend to go from bad to worse.

MURPHY'S FIFTH LAW: If there is a possibility of several things going wrong, the one that will cause the most damage will be the one.

MURPHY'S SIXTH LAW: Nature always sides with the hidden flaw.

MURPHY'S SEVENTH LAW: It always costs more than first estimated.

MURPHY'S EIGHTH LAW: If you try to please everybody, somebody will be disappointed.

MURPHY'S NINTH LAW: It is easier to get involved in something than to get out of it.

MURPHY'S TENTH LAW: Every solution breeds new problems.

MURPHY'S ELEVENTH LAW: Whenever you set out to do something, something else must be done first.

MURPHY'S TWELFTH LAW: If you perceive that there are four possible ways in which a procedure can go wrong and circumvent these, then a fifth way will promptly develop.

MURPHY'S THIRTEENTH LAW: If you're feeling good, don't worry; you'll get over it.

MURPHY'S FOURTEENTH LAW: It is impossible to make anything foolproof because fools are so ingenious.

MURPHY'S FIFTEENTH LAW: If you tinker with anything long enough, it will break.

MURPHY'S SIXTEENTH LAW: By making things absolutely clear, people will become confused.

MURPHY'S SEVENTEENTH LAW: The more complex the idea or technology, the more simpleminded is the opposition.

MURPHY'S EIGHTEENTH LAW: The more urgent the need for a decision, the less apparent becomes the identity of the decision maker.

MURPHY'S NINETEENTH LAW: If there is a 50 percent chance of success, that means there is a 75 percent chance of failure.

MURPHY'S TWENTIETH LAW: Interchangeable parts won't.

MURPHY'S TWENTY-FIRST LAW: In any computation, the figure that is obviously correct will be the source of error.

MURPHY'S TWENTY-SECOND LAW: Blame will never be placed if enough people are involved.

MURPHYS TWENTY-THIRD LAW: No matter what happens, someone will credit a pet theory.

MURPHY'S TWENTY-FOURTH LAW: A fail-safe circuit will destroy all others.

MURPHY'S SOCIAL THEORY: If in the course of several months only three worthwhile social events take place, they all will fall on the same evening.

MURPHY'S LAW OF THERMODYNAMICS: Things get worse under pressure.

MURPHY'S PHILOSOPHY: Smile—tomorrow will be worse.

My interest in Murphy's Laws aroused my curiosity about Murphy the *man*. I had always been assured that Murphy was a male engineer working for a large corporation, Xerox, GE, Lockheed, General Motors, IBM, etc., but when I made inquiries at these companies' factories, I was unable to obtain any information useful in my quest. Many employees had vague recollections of Murphy having worked in their divisions. "Oh, yes, Murphy—first name was Fred or was it Ed, short for Edsel? Used to work on quality control . . . or was it systems engineering? Used to say, 'All constants are variables.' Strange chap." But when I checked the files, there was no record of Edsel Murphy ever having been there. I believe that male chauvinism has blinded us to the obvious. Murphy is a woman. When Mrs. Murphy raised the lid from her pot of chowder and therein discovered a pair of overalls, her first utterance was: "Whatever can go wrong will go wrong."

PARKINSON'S LAWS

Parkinson's Law at twenty-one years of age is alive and well. Its thesis about the useless proliferation of bureaucracy probably has greater validity today than it did back in 1957, when C. Northcote Parkinson's first book [19] on the subject was published.

At that time he was teaching history at the University of Malaysia. He had gone to the British colony when Malaysia was preparing to become a new and independent country. Of course, this meant it had to have a new radio network, a new university, and a new history curriculum. Before long Parkinson found himself on thirty-two committees. It was during this period that he made many of his observations about committees. He organized these observations into a new scientific study he called committology. One of his findings about committee size tended to support the idea expressed in the old rhyme:

> Committees of twenty deliberate plenty,
> Committees of ten act now and then,
> But most jobs are done by committees of one.

As he reflected on Malaysian bureaucracy at work, he recalled his military experience as a staff officer in the Army during World War II. The idea occurred to him that in wartime you can build in two weeks an organizational structure that would take years to accumulate in peacetime. A bureaucracy can begin, grow, and proliferate so rapidly that the total process is more evident. Example: Somebody is needed to interpret aerial photographs, so a private is given the job. Two days later he is back, complaining that he needs another man to help him as there are too many photographs. He also requests a promotion to lance corporal in order that he may have authority over his helper. These reasonable requests are granted, and in three months he has a staff of eighty-five and he has become a lieutenant colonel, who never looks at another aerial photograph because he is too busy tending to administration.

Contemplation of these experiences led to writing an essay entitled "Parkinson's Law." It was submitted to *The Economist*, a serious journal, where its satirical view of bureaucracy was in sharp contrast with the rest of the magazine's content. The publication of "Parkinson's Law" in *The Economist* was a stroke of good fortune. The novelty of a humorous article in such an authoritative paper drew it immediately to the attention of the intellectual and business communities. Parkinson's reputation as a lawmaker was established. He retired from teaching and devoted his time to writing about bureaucracy, lecturing to business groups, discovering more laws, and indulging in his many interests, including painting, naval history, and the restoration of his medieval house and property on the island of Guernsey, where he now lives and works.

Parkinson's First Law and most of the books and laws that followed had to do with the useless expansion of manpower, finance, buildings, and so forth. It appears that Parkinsonian influences were in effect in ancient Egypt. The pyramids were the biggest structures man ever built, for the wrong reason.

When Hannibal crossed the Alps with his herds of war elephants, he believed that they would strike terror in the hearts of the enemy forces. But what really happened was that the giant beasts amused the opposing armies, particularly when they turned around and fled from the battle areas, tramping Hannibal's own soldiers. His packs of pachyderms continued to ruin his campaigns, but he went to his deathbed sighing, "Oh, if only I had more elephants."

PARKINSON'S FIRST LAW: Work expands to fill the time available for its completion.

Although general recognition of the truth of this statement had existed for a long time and had been explained in such proverbs as "If you want to get something done, ask a busy man to do it" or "It is the busiest man who has time to spare," it took the genius of Parkinson to identify it as a mathematically provable law with universal application. The essence of his discovery was that the number of employees in any public bureau tended to rise at an annual rate of about 6 percent, regardless of the amount of work to be done or even if no work was done.

He deduced the law from two self-evident truths: (1) An official wants to multiply subordinates, not rivals, and (2) officials make work for each other. Putting these rules into practice produces the following example.

Civil Servant A, thinking himself overworked, hires not just one assistant, B, who might become his possible successor, but two subordinates, C and D, dividing the work so that A will be the only man who comprehends both jobs.

As these individuals make work for each other, C, in turn, will find himself overworked and will demand and get two assistants of his own. A can then avoid internal friction only by advising the appointment of two more assistants to help D. Seven officials are now doing what one did before. These seven make so much work for each other that all are fully occupied and A is actually busier than ever.

The beauty of Parkinson's Law is that it predicts the rising pyramid of government bureaucracy and shows the inevitability of staff growth whether there is more work, less work, or none at all. A practical application of Parkinson's Law could be the accurate prediction of the exact time when all public and private productive activity in America will come to a complete halt. Since government bureaucracies are expanding at a calculable Parkinsonian rate far in excess of population growth, it is inevitable that a time will come when every citizen will be a government employee. Because government support is derived from taxes extracted from the private sector, at that point when the private sector disappears, government will do likewise.

PARKINSON'S SECOND LAW: Expenditures rise to meet income.

This law is obvious to anyone who has received a salary increase and then discovered that the extra money was silently absorbed, leaving the family's finances the same as they were before or perhaps even worse. This trend in individual finance becomes imperative when applied to government spending.

PARKINSON'S THIRD LAW: Expansion means complexity, and complexity means decay.

PARKINSON'S FOURTH LAW: The number of people in any working group tends to increase regardless of the amount of work to be done.

PARKINSON'S FIFTH LAW: If there is a way to delay an important decision, the good bureaucracy, public or private, will find it.

Axiom 1. An official wants to multiply subordinates, not rivals.
Axiom 2. Officials make work for each other.

PARKINSON'S SIXTH LAW: The progress of science varies inversely with the number of journals published.

MRS. PARKINSON'S LAW: Heat produced by pressure expands to fill the mind available, from which it can pass only to a cooler mind.

According to Parkinson, this law applies specifically to married women of the Western world. He contends that domestic disasters are caused by the emotional or physical heat generated by stress points in operating a household, such as getting the children off to school or preparing for dinner guests. This heat remains after the immediate cause has gone and builds up until an explosion occurs. The heat builds up because in the nuclear family there is nobody else to whom it can be transferred until her spouse appears on the scene.

PARKINSON'S EXPERIMENTAL LAW: Research expands to fill the space and time available for its completion and publication.

PARKINSON'S LAW FOR MEDICAL RESEARCH: Successful research attracts the bigger grant, which makes further research impossible.

PARKINSON'S LAW OF DELAY: Delay is the deadliest form of denial.

The abominable No-man is being replaced by the Prohibitive Procrastinator. Instead of saying No, the modern administrator practicing prohibitive procrastination says, "In due course." Through sufficient repetitions of this reply, over time he achieves negation by delay. It appears that the Law of Delay has been in effect for quite some time. The Roman Quintus Fabius Maximus (275–203 B.C.) was known as Cuncator, which means "the Delayer." He avoided direct engagement with, but kept harassing, the army of Hannibal, the Carthaginian general, until Hannibal finally gave up and went home.

PETER'S PRINCIPLES

There is general agreement that Sir Isaac Newton was the culminating figure of the seventeenth-century scientific revolution. One of his great contributions was his formulation of the Law of Gravitation. He claimed that the inspiration for this law came to him when he observed an apple fall from a tree toward the earth. Brilliant though this observation was, it took more than one law to explain gravitation. As a matter of fact, Newton's Laws tell us very little about apples except their tendency to be influenced by gravity (Newton apples are no exception).

When one considers the complexity and unreliability of human behavior in contrast with that of apples, is it any wonder that the social scientists in the law-writing business are compelled to write so many and such a variety of laws, principles, rules, theories, axioms, maxims, and ordinances in order to explain the human condition?

I first became involved in writing principles when I was doing a study of competence within a school system. As I studied the hierarchy, I observed that frequently a good student in teacher's college graduated to become a poor teacher— a competent consumer of knowledge promoted to incompetent dispenser of knowledge. I saw that sometimes a competent teacher was escalated to inadequate administrator—a competent educator of children promoted to incompetent manager of adults and so on. I called this phenomenon

THE PETER PRINCIPLE: In a hierarchy each employee tends to rise to his or her level of incompetence.[20]

It is a principle, not a law, because it is neither universal nor immutable. The principle only describes a tendency of most individuals to climb until they arrive at their levels of incapacity. There they remain, frustrating their coworkers and eroding the efficiency of the organization. The principle does not exclude the happy possibility that some competent teachers refuse promotion and stay in the classroom and that some artists, writers, craftsmen, and other individualists remain outside the hierarchy, where they regularly experience the joys of accomplishment that are seldom experienced by those who remain in the rat race.

Although the Peter Principle is not a law, it did get written into the law in the State of California. The courts ruled that a defendant had been subjected to the improper use of the Peter Principle.

The story has a happy ending, but it took a two-and-one-half-year battle for Doris Judd to get her job back in the campus cafeteria at the University of California. On February 4, 1973, she was fired from her food-services job as head sandwich maker for failing to spread the mayonnaise all the way to the edges of the bread.

Two courts found that the Mayonnaise Lady, so named by the California State Employees Association, had been unjustly fired. A Yolo County Superior Court decision reinstated her to the job with back pay. The Third District Court of Appeals in Sacramento unanimously upheld the reinstatement. The decision read: "Mrs. Judd's promotion to head of the sandwich department seems to have been a deliberate invocation of the Peter Principle done with the hope that she would provide her superiors with ample reasons to discharge her."

During the lengthy court battle someone else got the mayonnaise job, so Mrs. Judd was rehired to do hamburgers. She now works the grill and recently demonstrated her competence, during a noon rush, by satisfactorily preparing twelve dozen hamburgers, two dozen grilled-cheese sandwiches, and some patty melts.

This case established a legal precedent and provided a warning to employers. I have made a summary of these points and named it in Doris's honor in recognition of her long struggle to prove that she had been the innocent victim of the illegal invocation of the Peter Principle.

> JUDD'S LAW: It is managerial malpractice to use the Peter Principle intentionally as the means for dumping an employee.

In answering questions about the Peter Principle, I have used corollaries and specific principles that are subsets of the principle.

Corollary 1. Given enough time and assuming the existence of enough ranks in the hierarchy, each employee rises to, and remains at, his or her level of incompetence.

Corollary 2. In time, every post tends to be occupied by an employee who is incompetent to carry out its duties.

Corollary 3. Work is accomplished by those employees who have not yet reached their levels of incompetence.

Corollary 4. The cream rises until it sours.

Corollary 5. For every job that exists in the world, there is someone, somewhere, who can't do it. Given enough promotions, that incompetent will eventually get that job.

Corollary 6. A journey of 1,000 miles ends with but a single step.

PETER'S BUREAUCRATIC PRINCIPLE: Bureaucracy defends the status quo long past the time when the quo has lost its status.

PETER'S PRINCIPLE OF MANAGEMENT BY OBJECTIVE: If you don't know where you are going, you will end up somewhere else.

PETER'S THEORY OF RELEVANT KNOWLEDGE: Ignorance is no excuse—it's the real thing.

PETER'S THEOLOGICAL PRINCIPLE: Don't believe in miracles—depend on them.

PETER'S BUREAUCRATIC PERSPECTIVE: An incompetent in high office is like a man on a mountaintop; everything looks small to him, and he looks small to everyone else.

PETER'S CALCULATION: No executive devotes much effort to proving himself wrong.

PETER'S LAW OF PROBABILITY: When you are investigating the unknown, the outcomes are unpredictable.

PETER'S LEGAL FORMULA: Suppression is nine points of the law.

PETER'S THEORY OF SURVIVAL: Humankind may expand its place in creation only at its own risk.

PETER'S PRINCIPLE OF PEACE: A shaky peace is better than a steady war.

PETER'S PROGNOSIS: Spend sufficient time in confirming the need and the need will disappear.

PETER'S THEOREM: Incompetence plus incompetence equals incompetence.

PETER'S HYPOTHESIS: Man cannot live by incompetence alone.

PETER'S LAW OF SUBSTITUTION: Take care of the molehills and the mountains will take care of themselves.

PETER'S LAW OF RELIABILITY: Any system that depends on human reliability is unreliable.

PETER'S PLANNING PRINCIPLE: A poorly planned project takes four times longer to complete than expected, whereas a well-planned project takes only twice as long.

PETER'S LAW OF DISCOVERY: Most great discoveries are made by mistake, and the bigger the funding, the longer it takes to make that mistake.

PETER'S POLLYANNA PRINCIPLE: Nobody is ever a complete failure—he or she can always serve as a bad example.

PETER'S NONRECIPROCAL LAW OF PREDICTIONS: Negative predictions yield negative results; positive predictions yield negative results.

PETER'S THEORY OF EVOLUTION: Competence always contains the seeds of incompetence.

PETER'S PRINCIPLE OF BUREAUCRATIC LEADER-SHIP: The mark of bureaucratic leadership is the ability to assign jobs to those least able to do them.

PETER'S THEORY OF ENTREPRENEURIAL AGGRES-SIVENESS IN HIGHER EDUCATION: Competition in academia is so vicious because the stakes are so small.

PETER'S RULE OF PEAK EXPERIENCE: Climb the ladder of success, reach the top, and you'll find you're over the hill.

PETER'S LAW OF DENIAL: All of Peter's Principles may be bypassed if one learns the simple art of doing without thinking.

OTHER LAWS FROM A TO Z

ABBOTT'S SYSTEMS THEORY: A system is an ill-assorted collection of nonintegrated parts forming a chaotic whole.

ABEL'S CONSERVATIVE PRINCIPLE: Never do anything for the first time.

ACHESON'S BUREAUCRATIC RULE: A memorandum is written not to inform the reader but to protect the writer.

—DEAN ACHESON

ACTON'S RULE: Power tends to corrupt; absolute power corrupts absolutely.

—LORD ACTON

ADAMS'S LAW: There is no such thing as an underestimate of average intelligence.

—HENRY ADAMS

ADE'S LAW: Anybody can win, unless there happens to be a second entry.

—GEORGE ADE

ADLER'S MAXIM: The chief danger in life is that you may take too many precautions.

—ALFRED ADLER

ALCOTT'S LAW: To be ignorant of one's ignorance is the malady of the ignorant.

—BRONSON ALCOTT

ALLEN'S LAW: Almost anything is easier to get into than out of.

—AGNES ALLEN

ARISTOTLE'S AXIOM: The worst form of inequality is to try to make unequal things equal.

—ARISTOTLE

AUGUSTINE'S PRINCIPLE: A thing is not necessarily true because badly uttered, nor false because spoken magnificently.

—ST. AUGUSTINE

AUSTIN'S ENERGY THEORY: Children have more energy after a hard day of play than they do after a good night's sleep.

BACH'S CARDIAC PRINCIPLE: Don't worry about your heart, it will last you all of your life.

—DR. ALFRED BACH

BAKER'S LAW: Misery no longer loves company. Nowadays it insists on it.

BALZAC'S LAW: There is only one giant machine operated by pygmies, and that is bureaucracy.

—HONORÉ DE BALZAC

BARKLEY'S LAW: A bureaucrat is a Democrat who holds some office that a Republican wants.

—ALBEN W. BARKLEY

BARTH'S DISTINCTION: There are two types of people: those who divide people into two types and those who don't.

BARUCH'S RULE: Always do one thing less than you think you can do.

—BERNARD BARUCH

BARUCH'S THEORY: We didn't all come over on the same ship, but we're all in the same boat.

—BERNARD BARUCH

BEHAN'S LAW: There's no bad publicity, except an obituary notice.

—BRENDAN BEHAN

BENCHLEY'S LAW: Any man can do any amount of work, provided it isn't the work he's supposed to be doing.

—ROBERT BENCHLEY

BENN'S LAW: Liberty is being free from the things we don't like in order to be slaves of the things we do like.

—ERNEST BENN

BENNETT'S LAW: The moment you're born you're done for!

—ARNOLD BENNETT

BERENSON'S PRINCIPLE: Consistency requires you to be as ignorant today as you were a year ago.

—BERNARD BERENSON

BERRA'S SECOND LAW: Anyone who is popular is bound to be disliked.

—YOGI BERRA

BILLINGS'S LAW: *Silence is one of the hardest things to refute.*

—JOSH BILLINGS

BOOKER'S LAW: *An ounce of application is worth a ton of abstraction.*

BORE'S LAW: *Here today and here tomorrow.*

—BINNIE BARNES

BOREN'S RULE: *Nothing is impossible until it is sent to a committee.*

—JAMES H. BOREN

BORGE'S RULE: *Santa Claus has the right idea: Visit people once a year.*

—VICTOR BORGE

BOURNE'S LAW: *Never buy a dog and do your own barking.*

—HUMPHREY BOURNE

BOWLES'S LAW: *Government is too big and important to be left to the politicians.*

—CHESTER BOWLES

BRADSHAW'S COROLLARY TO THE PETER PRINCIPLE: *Work is delegated down to the level at which it cannot be competently carried out.*

—CHRISTOPHER BRADSHAW

BROUN'S LAW: *Appeasers believe that if you keep on throwing steaks to a tiger, the tiger will become a vegetarian.*

—HEYWOOD BROUN

BROWN'S LAW FOR CONSERVING ENERGY: *Ignore today's communiqué; tomorrow's will countermand it anyway.*

—LORRAINE BROWN

BUCY'S LAW: Nothing is ever accomplished by a reasonable man.

BUNK'S LAW: At any given time there are more important people in the world than important jobs to contain them.

—Bunk Carter

BUTLER'S CONCEPT: America is the best half-educated country in the world.

—Nicholas Murray Butler

BYRNES'S LAW: The nearest approach to immortality on earth is a government bureau.

—James Byrnes

CAHN'S AXIOM: When all else fails, read the instructions.

CAINE'S LAW OF PARTY PARITY: Anyone whom you meet at a party will automatically and without question assume your right to be there and your equal status with himself.

CAMUS'S LAW: To grow old is to pass from passion to compassion.

—Albert Camus

CAPONE'S LAW: You can get much farther with a kind word and a gun than you can with a kind word alone.

—Al Capone

CAPP'S THEORY: The closest you can get to your youth is to start repeatin' your follies.

—Andy Capp (Reg Smyth)

CARLYLE'S LAW: Every new opinion, at its starting, is precisely in a minority of one.

—Thomas Carlyle

CHESTERTON'S RULE: *It is better to speak wisdom foolishly like the saints than to speak folly wisely like the deans.*
—G. K. CHESTERTON

CHISHOLM'S LAW OF INEVITABILITY: *Any time things appear to be going better, you have overlooked something.*

CHEVALIER'S HYPOTHESIS: *Growing old isn't so bad when you consider the alternative.*
—MAURICE CHEVALIER

CIARDI'S THEORY: *The constitution gives every American the inalienable right to make a damn fool of himself.*
—JOHN CIARDI

CLEMENS'S PROPOSITION: *Experience teaches us only one thing at a time—and hardly that in my case.*
—MARK TWAIN

CLOPTON'S LAW: *For every credibility gap there is a gullibility fill.*
—DR. RICHARD CLOPTON

COBB'S LAW: *If writers were good businessmen, they'd have too much sense to be writers.*
—IRVIN S. COBB

COLE'S LAW: *Grated cabbage.*

COLLATERAL AXIOM: *In order to get a loan, you must first prove you don't need it.*

COMMUNICABLE DISEASE RULE: *A child can be exposed to mumps for weeks without catching it but can catch it without exposure the day before the family's vacation.*

CONRAD'S CONCEPT: *It is respectable to have no illusions, and safe and profitable and dull.*
—JOSEPH CONRAD

COOLIDGE'S FISCAL FORMULA: The secret of financial success is to buy sound stock, wait until it goes up and then sell it. If it does not go up, don't buy it.

—CALVIN COOLIDGE

COOPER'S LAW: All machines are amplifiers.

CORNFIELD'S LAW: It is morally wrong to allow suckers to keep their money.

COUGHLIN'S FIRST LAW: Don't speak unless you can improve the silence.

COUGHLIN'S SECOND LAW: In polite society, never open your mouth unless you have nothing to say.

COWARD'S CREDO: It doesn't matter how bold you are when the dangerous age is past.

—NOEL COWARD

CUSTER'S LAW: The point of no return is best achieved by overconfidence.

DARWIN'S INEXORABLE LAW: Happiness is not good for work.

—CHARLES DARWIN

DEFOE'S LAW: It is better to have a lion at the head of an army of sheep than a sheep at the head of an army of lions.

DeVRIES'S LAW: The hand that rules the cradle rocks the world.

—PETER DeVRIES

DIALECTICS OF PROGRESS RULE: Direct action produces direct reaction.

D'ISRAELI'S LAW: The defects of great men are the consolation of dunces.

—ISAAC D'ISRAELI

DOBBINS'S LAW: When in doubt, use a bigger hammer.

DOW'S LAW: In a hierarchal organization, the higher the level the greater the confusion.

DUNN'S LAW: Everything one does enough of eventually generates its own interest and one then begins to believe in it.

—ALAN DUNN

DURANT'S CONCEPT: To say nothing, especially when speaking, is half the art of diplomacy.

—WILL DURANT

DURANT'S RULE: Nothing is new except arrangement.

—WILL DURANT

EDISON'S MOTTO: I start where the last man left off.

—THOMAS ALVA EDISON

ELLIS'S LAW: What we call progress is the exchange of one nuisance for another nuisance.

—HAVELOCK ELLIS

EMERSON'S PERCEPTION: In every work of genius we recognize our rejected thoughts.

—RALPH WALDO EMERSON

EMERSON'S LAW: A weed is a plant whose virtues have not yet been discovered.

—RALPH WALDO EMERSON

ESAR'S LAW: Pick a winner. Anyone can pick the loser.

ESSLIN'S MOTTO: The dignity of man lies in his ability to face reality in all its senselessness.

—MARTIN ESSLIN

ETTORE'S LAW: The Other Line moves faster.

—BARBARA ETTORE

EXECUTIVE UMBRELLA LAW: A businessman needs three umbrellas—one to leave at the office, one to leave at home, and one to leave on the train.

EXTANT'S LAW: Any sufficiently advanced technology is indistinguishable from magic.

FALKLAND'S RULE: When it is not necessary to make a decision, it is necessary not to make a decision.

—LORD FALKLAND

FELDSTEIN'S LAW: Never play leapfrog with a unicorn.

FEUCHTWANGER'S LAW: There's only one step from the sublime to the ridiculous, but there's no road leading back from the ridiculous to the sublime.

—LION FEUCHTWANGER

FIEDLER'S LAW OF PREDICTION: Forecasting is very difficult—especially if it's about the future.

—EDGAR FIEDLER

FINAGLE FACTOR: The Finagle Factor is a variable statistic that can be employed in any calculation to bring actual results without the necessity of repeating messy experiments, studies, or reviews of data.

FINAGLE'S FIRST LAW: The likelihood of a thing's happening is inversely proportional to its desirability.

FINAGLE'S SECOND LAW: Once a job is fouled up, anything done to improve it only makes it worse.

FISCHER'S LAW: A conclusion is the place where you got tired thinking.

—MARTIN H. FISCHER

FITZGERALD'S PRECEPT: Few people make all of life's journey on a green light.

—DR. ERNEST A. FITZGERALD

FLO CAPP'S THEORY OF AGGRAVATION: If there's one thing worse than being wrong, it's being right with nobody listening.

—MRS. ANDY CAPP (REG SMYTH)

FORBES'S FORMULA: There is more satisfaction in being a first-rate truck driver than in being a tenth-rate executive.

—B. C. FORBES

FORRESTER'S LAW: In complicated situations efforts to improve things often make them worse, sometimes much worse, on occasion calamitous.

FRANCE'S LAW: The future is hidden even from the men who make it.

—ANATOLE FRANCE

FRANKEL'S LAW: Whatever happens in government could have happened differently, and it usually would have been better if it had.

FREUD'S RULE: Heads I win, tails you lose!

—SIGMUND FREUD

FROMM'S THEORY: The danger of the past was that men became slaves. The danger of the future is that men may become robots.

—ERICH FROMM

FROST'S THEORY: Pressed into service means pressed out of shape.

—ROBERT FROST

GAINES'S LAW: If you want to publish a consistently funny magazine it is best to be a total eccentric.

—WILLIAM MAXWELL GAINES
(publisher of *Mad* magazine)

GANE'S RULE: Everything put together falls apart eventually.

GANDHI'S LAW: Take care of the means, and the end will take care of itself.

—MAHATMA GANDHI

GARDNER'S LAW: Success is getting what you want, and happiness is wanting what you get.

—DAVE GARDNER

GILBERT'S LAW: When everyone is somebody, then no one's anybody.

—SIR W. S. GILBERT

GINSBERG'S THEOREM:
 1. You can't win.
 2. You can't break even.
 3. You can't even get out of the game.

GLASSER'S LAW: There are only two places in our world where time takes precedence over the job to be done: school and prison.

—WILLIAM GLASSER

GOETHE'S LAW: To rule is easy, to govern difficult.
—JOHANN WOLFGANG VON GOETHE

GOLDSMITH'S LAW: Every absurdity has a champion to defend it.

—OLIVER GOLDSMITH

GOMEZ'S LAW: If you don't throw it, they can't hit it.
—LEFTY GOMEZ

GRESHAM'S LAW: Trivial matters are handled promptly; important matters are never solved.

GUMPERTZ'S LIBRARY LAW: The pertinent page is the one that is torn out.

——JENNY GUMPERTZ

GUNDLACH HYPOTHESIS: The probability of, and resulting cost of, incompetence increases in direct proportion to the size of the hierarchy.

——CHRIS GUNDLACH

HALBERSTAM'S HUNCH: The things that bother a press about a President will ultimately bother the country.

——DAVID HALBERSTAM

HAMILTON'S LAW: Man is a reasoning rather than a reasonable animal.

——ALEXANDER HAMILTON

HARRIS'S PRINCIPLE: The real danger is not that men will begin to think like men, but that men will begin to think like computers.

——SIDNEY J. HARRIS

HARTLEY'S LAW: Never sleep with anyone crazier than yourself.

HARUM'S AXIOM: The only man who can change his mind is a man that's got one.

——DAVID HARUM (E. N. WESTCOTT)

HARVARD'S FIRST LAW: Under the most rigorously controlled conditions of pressure, temperature, volume, humidity, and other variables, the organism will do as it damn well pleases.

HARVARD'S SECOND LAW: The sum of intelligence on the planet is a constant; the population is growing.

HAYAKAWA'S RULE: Agreement is brought about by changing people's minds—other people's.

——S. I. HAYAKAWA

HELLER'S LAW: The first myth of management is that it exists.

—ROBERT HELLER

HEMINGWAY'S THEORY: What is moral is what you feel good after.

—ERNEST HEMINGWAY

HENDRICKSON'S LAW: If you have enough meetings over a long enough period of time, the meetings become more important than the problems the meetings were intended to solve.

HENRY'S LAW: Nice guys don't finish nice.

HENTOFF'S LAW: The white man's burden is himself.

—NAT HENTOFF

HEROLD'S LAW: Unhappiness is not knowing what we want and killing ourselves to get it.

—DON HEROLD

HIGGINS'S HYPOTHESIS: There's no such thing as a little garlic.

HIGGINS'S LAW: Everything goes to hell if you wait long enough.

HIGG'S THEOREM: If it looks easy, it's tough. If it looks tough, it's damn well impossible.

HITLER'S LAW: The bigger the lie, the harder they fall.

HOARE'S LAW OF PROBLEM SOLVING: Inside every large problem there is a small problem struggling to get out.

HOFFER'S LAW: When people are free to do as they please, they usually imitate each other.

—ERIC HOFFER

HOFFER'S PREDICTION: People who bite the hand that feeds them usually lick the boot that kicks them.

—ERIC HOFFER

HORNER'S FIVE-THUMB POSTULATE: Experience gained is proportionate to the amount of equipment ruined.

HOWE'S THEORY: There is some advice that is too good —the advice to love your enemies, for example.

—ED HOWE

HUNT'S RULE OF ENGINEERING DESIGN: Never design anything the plant is not already equipped to build.

—LLOYD F. HUNT

HULL'S THEORY: He who trims himself to suit everybody will soon whittle himself away.

—RAYMOND HULL

HUROK'S LAW: If people don't want to come, nothing will stop them.

—SOL HUROK

HURST'S HYPOTHESIS: A woman has to be twice as good as a man to go half as far.

—FANNIE HURST

HUTCHINS'S RULE: It is not so important to be serious as it is to be serious about important things.

—ROBERT MAYNARD HUTCHINS

HUXLEY'S PROVERB: Ye shall know the truth, and the truth shall make you mad.

—ALDOUS HUXLEY

IBM POLLYANNA PRINCIPLE: Machines should work; people should think.

INHOFF'S LAW: The organization of any bureaucracy is

very much like a septic tank. The really big chunks always rise to the top.

IRVING'S RULE: *The bigger they are, the harder they fall.*

—CLIFFORD IRVING

ISSAWI'S LAW OF SOCIAL MOTION: *A shortcut is the longest distance between two points.*

—CHARLES ISSAWI

ISSAWI'S DEVELOPMENT RULE: *In an undeveloped country, when you are absent, your job is taken away from you; in a developed country, a new one is piled on you.*

—CHARLES ISSAWI

JACKSON'S LAW: *No one is ever old enough to know better.*

—HOLBROOK JACKSON

JAY'S FIRST LAW: *The classic hierarchy consists of one man at the top with three below him, each of whom has three below him, and so on with fearful symmetry unto the seventh generation, by which stage there is a row of 729 managers.*

JOHNSON'S LAW OF AUTO REPAIR: *Any tool dropped while being used to repair an automobile will roll on the floor to the exact geographic center of the vehicle's undercarriage.*

JAMES'S LAW: *There is no greater lie than a truth misunderstood.*

—WILLIAM JAMES

JEFFREYS'S LAW: *The defendant is entitled to a fair trial before I hang him.*

—HANGING JUDGE JEFFREYS

JENKINSON'S LAW: *It won't work.*

JIM BRADY'S LAW: Eat, drink and be merry, and tomorrow you'll be a fat, grinning drunkard.

JOHN BIRCH'S LAW: Flying saucers are real. The Air Force doesn't exist.

JONG'S LAW: Advice is what we ask for when we already know the answer but wish we didn't.

—ERICA JONG

JUNG'S PRINCIPLE: Medicines cure diseases, but doctors cure patients.

—CARL JUNG

KENNEDY'S CONSTANT: Don't get mad—get even.
—JOHN F. KENNEDY

KENNEDY'S PRINCIPLE: Washington is a city of Southern efficiency and Northern charm.

—JOHN F. KENNEDY

KHARASCH'S AXIOMS OF INSTITUTIONAL ACTION:

First Axiom: Any institutional action is merely the working of the institution's internal machinery.

Second Axiom: Institutional existence depends upon the continual working of the internal machinery.

Third Axiom: Whatever the internal machinery does is perceived within the institution as the real purpose of the institution (i.e., function is seen as purpose).

—ROBERT N. KHARASCH

KHARASCH'S INSTITUTIONAL IMPERATIVE: Every action or decision of an institution must be intended to keep the institutional machinery working.

Corollary: To speak of any goal or purpose of an institution other than keeping the institutional machinery running is no more meaningful than to speak of the goal of an automobile exhaust or the purpose of the hum of a sewing machine.

—ROBERT N. KHARASCH

KHARASCH'S LAW OF INSTITUTIONAL EXPERTISE: The expert judgment of an institution, when the matter involves continuation of the institution's operations, is totally predictable (and hence totally worthless).

—ROBERT N. KHARASCH

KHARASCH'S LAW OF THE INSTITUTIONAL IRRELEVANCE OF TRUTH: When the making of a statement is seen as necessary to the continued working of the institutional machinery, the statement is totally predictable and its truth is irrelevant.

—ROBERT N. KHARASCH

KHARASCH'S LAW OF THE INSTITUTIONAL IRRELEVANCE OF MORALITY AND HUMANITY: If the operation of the institutional machinery requires an action, morality and humanity are irrelevant.

—ROBERT N. KHARASCH

KHARASCH'S SPECIAL LAW OF THE SECURITY OFFICE: The finding of threats to security by the security office is totally predictable, and hence the finding is totally worthless.

—ROBERT N. KHARASCH

KIERKEGAARD'S LAW: People demand freedom of speech to make up for the freedom of thought which they avoid.

—SÖREN AABE KIERKEGAARD

KINSEY'S LAW: The only unnatural sex act is that which you cannot perform.

—ALFRED KINSEY

KISH'S LAW: If it tastes good already, it's even better with paprika, sour cream, mushrooms, egg, onion, or garlic.

KITMAN'S LAW: Pure drivel tends to drive ordinary drivel off the TV screen.

—MARVIN KITMAN

KNEBEL'S LAW: Find a man with both feet firmly on the ground and you've found a man about to make a difficult putt.

—FLETCHER KNEBEL

KOMMEN'S LAW: If you look like your passport photo, you're too ill to travel.

—WILL KOMMEN

KUBIN'S MAXIM OF TOTAL RECALL: How feeble are Man's efforts against the unyielding forces of Nature—until the struggle is recounted for the grandchildren.

—JEANETTE KUBIN

LAW OF AMERICAN GRAFFITI: Research statistics are reliable, if you don't count on them.

LAW OF ENTREPRENEURIAL DESIGN: Every man has a scheme that will not work.

LAW OF PREDICTABLE RESULTS: No matter what happens, there is someone who knew it would.

LEE'S LAW: Never saw off the branch you are on, unless you are being hanged from it.

—STANISLAW J. LEE

LEVANT'S LAW: Strip away the phony tinsel of Hollywood and you find the real tinsel underneath.

—OSCAR LEVANT

LEVINSON'S HAIRLINE THEORY: No matter how well a toupee blends in back, in front it always looks like hell.

—LEONARD LOUIS LEVINSON

LEVY'S LAW: Only God can make a random selection.

LICHTENBERG'S HYPOTHESIS: In the future the so-called Dark Ages will perhaps be lengthened to include our own.

—GEORG CHRISTOPH LICHTENBERG

LICHTENBERG'S SAFETY LAW: The fly that doesn't want to get swatted is most secure when it lights on the flyswatter.

—GEORG CHRISTOPH LICHTENBERG

LINCOLN'S LAW: The best way to get a bad law repealed is to enforce it strictly.

—ABRAHAM LINCOLN

LINCOLN'S PRINCIPLE: I'd rather fail in a cause that will ultimately succeed than succeed in a cause that will ultimately fail.

—ABRAHAM LINCOLN

LIPPMANN'S LAW: Where all think alike, no one thinks very much.

—WALTER LIPPMAN

LIZZIE BORDEN'S LAW: Any job worth doing is worth doing well.

LLOYD GEORGE'S PRINCIPLE: Don't be afraid to take a big step if one is indicated; you can't cross a chasm in two small jumps.

—DAVID LLOYD GEORGE

LOWERY'S LAW: If it jams, force it. If it breaks, it needed replacing anyway.

LUCE'S LAW: No good deed goes unpunished.

—CLARE BOOTHE LUCE

LYND'S LAW: Life is worth living, but only if we avoid the amusements of grown-up people.

—ROBERT LYND

McPHERSON'S LAW: McPherson's bread always falls jelly side down.

MAGARY'S LAW: Computers can figure out all kinds of problems, except the things in the world that just don't add up.

—JAMES F. MAGARY

MAO'S LAW: The journey of a thousand miles begins with a single step.

—MAO TSE-TUNG

MARTIN'S LAW OF COMMUNICATION: The inevitable result of improved and enlarged communication between different levels in a hierarchy is a vastly increased area of misunderstanding.

—THOMAS L. MARTIN, JR.

MARX'S THEORY: Military intelligence is a contradiction in terms.

—GROUCHO MARX

MASSON'S MAXIM: "Be yourself" is the worst advice you can give to some people.

MAUGHAM'S LAW: Art for art's sake makes no more sense than gin for gin's sake.

—SOMERSET MAUGHAM

MEACHAM'S MAXIM: In a few seconds a computer can make a mistake so great that it would take many men many months to equal it.

—MERLE L. MEACHAM

MENCKEN'S EDUCATIONAL LAW:
> *Those who can do.*
> *Those who cannot do teach.*
> *Those who cannot teach administrate.*

MENCKEN'S LAW: It may be a sin to think evil of people, but it is seldom a mistake.

—H. L. MENCKEN

MENCKEN'S RULE: There is always an easy solution to every human problem—neat, plausible, and wrong.

—H. L. MENCKEN

MESKIMEN'S LAW OF PERFECTION: There is never time to do it right but always time to do it over.

MILL'S LAW: The perpetual obstacle to all human advancement is custom.

—JOHN STUART MILL

MILLER'S LAW: Exceptions prove the rule—and wreck the budget.

—OLIN MILLER

LES MISERABLES METALAW: All laws, whether good, bad, or indifferent, must be obeyed to the letter.

MONTAGU'S GENERALIZATION: Generalizations are generally wrong.

—MARY WORTLEY MONTAGU

MORROW'S LAW: The world is divided into people who do things and people who get the credit.

—DWIGHT MORROW

MOSELEY'S EXTENSION OF THE PETER PRINCIPLE: Executive behavior is based on the managerial myth that future organizational expansion will resolve past institutional incompetence.

—DOUG MOSELEY

MUMFORD'S MAXIM: Traditionalists are pessimists about the future and optimists about the past.

—LEWIS MUMFORD

MURROW'S LAW: The obscure we see eventually; the completely apparent takes longer.

—EDWARD R. MURROW

MUSHROOM PRINCIPLE: Keep them in the dark and feed them a little horse manure periodically.

MYRDAL'S LAW: Nineteen fresh apples do not make a single rotten apple fresh.

—GUNNAR MYRDAL

NAPOLEON'S THEORY: In politics, an absurdity is not a handicap.

—NAPOLEON BONAPARTE

NASH'S LAW: Progress might have been all right once, but it went on too long.

—OGDEN NASH

NELSON'S LAW: Now is the time for all good men to come to the aid of themselves.

—FELICE NELSON

NEWTON'S SEVENTH LAW: A bird in the hand is safer than one overhead.

NEWTON'S METALAW: For every law there is an equal and opposite law.

O'BRIEN'S $357.73 PRINCIPLE: Auditors always reject any expense account with a bottom line divisible by five or ten.

OLGA'S LAW: It's no fun being sick when you don't feel well.

—OLGA SHOAFF

OSBORNE'S LAW: *Variables won't; constants aren't.*

OSLER'S LAW: *There is a tendency for the person in the most powerful position in an organization to spend all of his time serving on committees and signing letters.*

—WILLIAM OSLER

PALLESEN'S PARADOX: *The more particular and painstaking the preparation of published precepts, the less likely they will precipitate the predicted pattern of performance or production.*

—PETER J. PALLESEN

PARKER'S RULE OF PARLIAMENTARY PROCEDURE: *A motion to adjourn is always in order.*

PASCAL'S LAW: *Nature is an infinite sphere whose center is everywhere and whose circumference is nowhere.*

—BLAISE PASCAL

PAUL'S LAW: *You can't fall off the floor.*

PAULSEN'S PRINCIPLE OF WOMEN'S LIBERATION: *No person should be denied equal rights because of the shape of her skin.*

—PAT PAULSEN

PEDDIWELL'S LAW OF ADMINISTRATIVE PARSIMONY: *With allowance for individual differences, a period of three to six years is enough time to spend on any administrative level in preparation for a more advanced job.*

—HAROLD R. W. BENJAMIN

PEER'S LAW: *The solution to a problem changes the problem.*

PERSONAL JUSTICE PRINCIPLE: *Everyone should get what's coming to him, without getting what he deserves.*

PERVERSITY OF NATURE LAW: You cannot success-fully determine beforehand which side of the bread to butter.

PETER PAN'S ECONOMIC PRINCIPLE: If I say, "I be-lieve, I believe, I believe," the economy will fly.
—ADAM SMITH

PETER'S ACCURACY PRINCIPLE: When working to-ward the solution for a problem, it always helps if you know the answer beforehand.

PETER'S ACCURACY TIMETABLE. Nothing can be totaled correctly after 4:37 P.M. on Friday.

PETER'S FIRST AMENDMENT AMENDMENT: What this country needs is more free speech worth listening to.

PETER'S CANONIZATION LAW: Paths of glory lead but to the grave—so do all other paths.

PETER'S CHARISMATIC LEADERSHIP FORMULA: Ascendance comes to those who can blow their own horn while blowing others' minds.

PETER'S COROLLARY TO WILL ROGERS'S PRINCI-PLE: I never met a yesman I didn't like.

PETER'S DIFFERENTIAL DIAGNOSIS: There are two kinds of losers: (1) the good loser and (2) those who can't act.

PETER'S DIAGNOSTIC RULE: Don't disagree with your doctor—he has inside information.

PETER'S EDUCATIONAL THEORY: Experience is the worst teacher—it gives the test before explaining the lesson.

PETER'S FINANCIAL PRINCIPLE: Starting from scratch is easy; starting without it is tough.

PETER'S FIRST RULE OF GRAMMAR: Don't use no double negatives.

PETER'S FORMULA FOR PERSONNEL EVALUATION: Anticipate and base judgments of others on your hierarchal superior's opinions.

PETER'S FINANCIAL REVELATION: After a raise in salary you will have less money at the end of each month than you had before.

PETER'S GOLDEN RULE: Those with the gold make the rules.

PETER'S INEVITABILITY PRINCIPLE: Live each day as if it were your last—and eventually you'll be right.

PETER'S LAUGH-IN PRINCIPLE: When the boss tells a joke, he who laughs lasts.

PETER'S LAW OF PROBABILITY: When you are investigating the unknown, the outcomes are unpredictable.

PETER'S LAW OF MODERN MEDICINE: The more effective the prescription, the more horrendous the side effects.

PETER'S MARRIAGE PRINCIPLE: All marriages are happy, but living together afterward can be troublesome.

PETER'S MAXIM: There is no rest for the wicked and damn little for the righteous.

PETER'S MEDICAL PRESCRIPTION: For the person who has everything—antibiotics.

PETER'S MEDICAL PROPHECY: The major side effect of medical treatment is bankruptcy.

PETER'S PLACEBO: An ounce of image is worth a pound of performance.

PETER'S POLITICAL PRINCIPLE: *Politicians make strange bedfellows, but they all share the same bunk.*

PETER'S PREPARATORY PRINCIPLE: *A stitch in time saves embarrassment.*

PETER'S PRESCRIPTION: *Quit while you are behind.*

PETER'S PRINCIPLE OF AGING: *Don't worry about middle age—you'll outgrow it.*

PETER'S PRINCIPLE OF PUBLIC INFORMATION: *Improvements in mass communication produce vastly increased areas of misunderstanding.*

PETER'S PROPHECY: *The meek shall inherit the earth, but not the oil rights.*

PETER'S PROPOSAL: *Anything worth doing is worth getting someone else to do.*

PETER'S PROPOSITION: *If you can't understand it, name it.*

PETER'S ROUTING FORMULA: *In government bureaucracies, difficult inquiries get passed to the lowest level of obscurity.*

PETER'S RULE ABOUT RULES: *Nobody ever breaks a rule until somebody makes one.*

PETER'S STONED PRINCIPLE: *Reality is for people who can't face drugs.*

PETER'S SURVIVAL PRINCIPLE: *Lead, follow, or get out of the way.*

PETER'S TAXATION PRINCIPLE: *Build a better mousetrap, and the government will build a better mousetrap tax.*

PETER'S TESTING PRINCIPLE: *Aptitude tests show that you will succeed in a business where your father is the boss.*

PETER'S THEORY OF RECIPROCAL INHIBITION OF FISCAL RECALL: Lending money to friends causes them to lose their memories.

PETER'S THEORY OF RELATIVITY: The red light is always longer than the green light.

PETER'S ULTIMATE INQUIRY: The question is: "Why does anything exist?"

PETER'S UNIVERSAL LAW: The expansion of the universe is due to the proliferation of universal laws.

MRS. PETER'S FIRST LAW OF HOUSEKEEPING: Dust breeds.

MRS. PETER'S SECOND LAW OF HOUSEKEEPING: Clutter expands to fill the space available.

MRS. PETER'S THIRD LAW OF HOUSEKEEPING: A man's home is his hassle.

MRS. PETER'S FOURTH LAW OF HOUSEKEEPING: 'Tis better to have loved and lost than to end up doing dishes twenty times a week.

MRS. PETER'S PAST, PRESENT, AND FUTURE RULE: You can't change the past, but you can ruin the present by worrying about the future.

PHILLIPPI'S LAW: There is a 50/50 chance of anything, because either it will or it won't.

—HANK PHILLIPPI

PICASSO'S PRINCIPLE: Art is the lie that enables us to realize the truth.

—PABLO PICASSO

PITKIN'S LAW: It is physically impossible for anybody to act intelligently even one-tenth as often as to act stupidly.

—WALTER PITKIN

PITT'S LAW: Where law ends, tyranny begins.

—WILLIAM PITT

POINT OF NO RETURN LAW: The light at the end of the tunnel could be the headlight of an oncoming train.

PFEIFFER'S RULE: Even vagueness can be explicit if it is explained well enough.

—DR. EDWARD J. PFEIFFER

POKER RULE No. 1: A Smith and Wesson beats four aces.

POKER RULE No. 2: Two deuces and a razor beat a full house.

POLITICAL EXPEDIENCY PRINCIPLE: If you can fool all of the people some of the time, that's enough.

POPE'S LAW: All looks yellow to a jaundiced eye.

—ALEXANDER POPE

PORTER'S LAW: The delay and expense involved in any action soar in perpendicular proportion to the number of approvals essential to take that action.

—SYLVIA PORTER

PRICE'S FIRST LAW: If everybody doesn't want it, nobody gets it.

—ROGER PRICE

PRINCIPLE OF MULTIFUNCTIONAL DEVICES: The fewer functions any device is required to perform, the more perfectly it can perform those functions.

PRINCIPLE OF RESEARCH: Never replicate a successful experiment.

PROBABILITY THEORY: The person holding the most tickets has the best chance of winning.

PUDDER'S LAW: Anything that begins well ends badly.

RAMO'S RULE (EXPERIMENTALLY OBSERVED UNIVERSAL LAW): At any given time in any organization the tendency towards incompetence exceeds the tendency towards competence.

Corollary 1. If some people are getting better, then more are getting worse.

Corollary 2. More competent people resign than incompetent people are fired.

Corollary 3. Some good qualities in people develop with time, but more bad ones get worse.

Corollary 4. The potentially competent tend to lose their potential with time while the potentially incompetent never fail to rise to their full expectations.

—SIMON RAMO

RAWLS'S LAW: Equality of opportunity insures an equal chance to leave the less fortunate behind.

RAYBURN'S PRINCIPLE: If you want to get along, go along.

—SAM RAYBURN

RAYBURN'S RULE: When you get too big a majority, you're immediately in trouble.

—SAM RAYBURN

RENARD'S RULE: Look for the absurd in everything and you will find it.

—JULES RENARD

REYNOLDS'S RULE: There is no expedient to which a man will not resort to avoid the real labor of thinking.

—SIR JOSHUA REYNOLDS

RESTON'S PRINCIPLE: The ship of state is the only known vessel that leaks from the top.

—JAMES RESTON

RICKOVER'S LAW: If the Russians would send a man to hell, we'd say, "We can't let them beat us to it."

—ADMIRAL H. RICKOVER

ROBERT'S LAW OF POLITICS: It is easier to be a liberal a long way from home.

ROBINSON'S LAW: The guy you beat out of a prime parking spot is the one you have to see for a job interview.

—CAL ROBINSON

ROGERS'S LAW: There is very little to admire in bureaucracy but you have got to hand it to the Internal Revenue Service.

—JAMES L. ROGERS

ROGERS'S RULE: In filling out an income tax return, let an accountant instead of your conscience be your guide.

—WILL ROGERS

ROOSEVELT'S RULE: When you get to the end of your rope, tie a knot and hang on.

—FRANKLIN DELANO ROOSEVELT

MRS. ROOSEVELT'S LAW: No one can make you feel inferior without your consent.

—ELEANOR ROOSEVELT

RUNYON'S RULE: The race is not always to the swift, nor the battle to the strong—but that's the way to bet.

—DAMON RUNYON

RUSSELL'S LAW: The whole is always worth less than the sum of its parts.

—DAVID RUSSELL

RUSSELL'S RULE: If fifty million people say a foolish thing, it is still a foolish thing.

—BERTRAND RUSSELL

RUSSELL'S THEORY: Science is what you know, philosophy is what you don't know.

—BERTRAND RUSSELL

SAHL'S LAW OF DESTINY: The future lies ahead.

—MORT SAHL

SANTAYANA'S FIRST LAW: Sanity is madness put to good use.

—GEORGE SANTAYANA

SANTAYANA'S SECOND LAW: When men and women agree, it is only in their conclusions; their reasons are always different.

—GEORGE SANTAYANA

SANTAYANA'S THIRD LAW: It takes a wonderful brain and exquisite senses to produce a few stupid ideas.

—GEORGE SANTAYANA

SCHMIDT'S SYSTEMS THEORY: Build a system that even a fool can use, and only a fool will want to use it.

SCHNITZLER'S LAW: Pretending that you believe a liar is also a lie.

—ARTHUR SCHNITZLER

SCHOPENHAUER'S LAW: Every nation ridicules other nations, and all are right.

—ARTHUR SCHOPENHAUER

SEVAREID'S LAW: The chief cause of problems is solutions.

—ERIC SEVAREID

SHALIT'S LAW: The intensity of movie publicity is in inverse proportion to the quality of the movie.

—GENE SHALIT

SHANAHAN'S LAW: The length of a meeting rises with the square of the number of people present.

SHAW'S HYPOTHESIS: Nothing is ever accomplished by a reasonable man.

—GEORGE BERNARD SHAW

SHAW'S LAW: The Good Old Days were neither better nor worse than the ones we're living through right now.

—ARTIE SHAW

SHAW'S PRINCIPLE OF POLITICAL PATRONAGE: A government that robs Peter to pay Paul can always depend on the support of Paul.

—GEORGE BERNARD SHAW

SHAW'S PROFESSIONAL COLLUSION PRINCIPLE: All professions are conspiracies against the laity.

—GEORGE BERNARD SHAW

SHEARER'S MAXIM OF UNDERSTANDING: The length of an explanation is indirectly proportional to the explainer's knowledge of the facts.

—AL SHEARER

SIPORIN'S MAXIM: Jumping to conclusions seldom leads to happy landings.

—STEVE SIPORIN

SITWELL'S THEORY: The public will believe anything, so long as it is not founded on the truth.

—EDITH SITWELL

SLOAN'S LAW: The changes in new models should be so

novel and attractive as to create dissatisfaction with past models.

—ALFRED SLOAN

SMITH'S HYGIENIC PRINCIPLE: *Cleanliness is next to impossible.*

—JACK SMITH

SMITH'S LITERARY PRINCIPLE: *When someone has the wit to coin a useful phrase, it ought to be acclaimed and broadcast or it will perish.*

—JACK SMITH

SOCIOGENETIC FIRST PRINCIPLE: *Celibacy is not hereditary.*

SOCRATES'S PRINCIPLE: *The unexamined life is not worth living.*

—SOCRATES

SOPHOCLES'S LAW: *A fool cannot be a good actor, but a good actor can act the fool.*

—SOPHOCLES

STEIN'S LAW: *Remarks aren't literature.*

—GERTRUDE STEIN

STEINMETZ'S PRINCIPLE: *No man really becomes a fool until he stops asking questions.*

—CHARLES P. STEINMETZ

STERN'S MAXIM: *Experience is a comb life gives you after you lose your hair.*

—JUDITH STERN

STEVENSON'S CONCEPT: *My definition of a free society is a society where it is safe to be unpopular.*

—ADLAI STEVENSON

STURGEON'S LAW: Ninety percent of everything is crud.

SWARTZBERG'S RULE: Never let well enough alone.

—IRVIN SWARTZBERG

TAILGATER'S SAFETY RULE: Don't drive on a highway where careless motorists are driving too close ahead of you.

TERMAN'S LAW OF INNOVATION: If you want a track team to win the high jump, you find one person who can jump seven feet, not seven people who can each jump one foot.

THEORY OF COMMUNICATION: I know you believe you understand what you think I said. But I am not sure you realize that what you heard is not what I meant.

THEORY OF GOOD SPORTSMANSHIP: It isn't whether you win or lose but how you place the blame.

THOREAU'S FIRST LAW: It is as hard to see oneself as to look backwards without turning around.

—HENRY DAVID THOREAU

THOREAU'S SECOND LAW: Men have become the tools of their tools.

—HENRY DAVID THOREAU

THOREAU'S THIRD LAW: The little things of life are as interesting as the big ones.

—HENRY DAVID THOREAU

THURBER'S LAW: It is better to have loafed and lost than never to have loafed at all.

—JAMES THURBER

THURBER'S THEORY: A pinch of probability is worth a pound of perhaps.

—JAMES THURBER

TOFFLER'S CONCEPT OF MANAGEMENT: The management of change is the effort to convert certain possibles into probables, in pursuit of agréed preferables.

—ALVIN TOFFLER

TROUT'S LAW: We are healthy only to the extent that our ideas are humane.

—KILGORE TROUT (KURT VONNEGUT, JR.)

TRUMAN'S LAW: You don't set a fox to guard the chickens just because he has a lot of experience in the hen house.

—HARRY TRUMAN

TWAIN'S FIRST LAW: It is easier to stay out than to get out.

—MARK TWAIN

TWAIN'S SECOND LAW: A man with a new idea is a crank until the idea succeeds.

—MARK TWAIN

TWO-RULE PROTOCOL OF JOB SECURITY: (1) The boss is always right. (2) When the boss is wrong, refer to Rule 1.

VALÉRY'S LAW: An artist never really finishes his work; he merely abandons it.

—PAUL VALÉRY

VALÉRY'S PRINCIPLE: The trouble with our time is that the future is not what is used to be.

—PAUL VALÉRY

VALÉRY'S RULE: History is the science of what never happens twice.

—PAUL VALÉRY

VOLTAIRE'S MAXIM: Doubt is not a pleasant mental state, but certainty is a ridiculous one.

—VOLTAIRE

VONNEGUT'S LAW: Things are going to get worse and worse and never get better again.

—KURT VONNEGUT, JR.

WALPOLE'S LAW: Foolish writers and readers are created for each other.

—HORACE WALPOLE

WEILER'S LAW: Nothing is impossible for the man who doesn't have to do it himself.

WEST'S LAW: To err is human, but it feels divine.

—MAE WEST

WESTCOTT'S LAW: There's about as much human nature in some folks as there is in others, if not more.

—EDWARD NOYES WESTCOTT

WHITE'S FIRST LAW: Security declines as security machinery expands.

—E. B. WHITE

WHITE'S SECOND LAW: An intelligence service is, in fact, a stupidity service.

—E. B. WHITE

WIKER'S LAW: Government expands to absorb revenue and then some.

WILDE'S GUIDE: A man cannot be too careful in the choice of his enemies.

—OSCAR WILDE

WILDE'S PERSONALITY THEORY: Only the shallow know themselves.

—OSCAR WILDE

WING WALKER'S FIRST LAW: Never leave hold of what you're got until you've got hold of something else.

WITZENBURG'S LAW OF AIRLINE TRAVEL: The distance between the ticket counter and your flight gate is directly proportionate to the weight of your luggage and inversely proportionate to the time remaining before takeoff.

WOOD'S LAW: Whatever you eat will kill you if you live long enough.

—JIM WOOD

WRIGHT'S FIRST LAW: The only thing wrong with architecture are the architects.

—FRANK LLOYD WRIGHT

WRIGHT'S SECOND LAW: A doctor can bury his mistakes, but an architect can only advise his client to plant vines.

—FRANK LLOYD WRIGHT

XAVIER'S THEORY OF THE BENT TWIG: Give me the children until they are seven and anyone may have them afterward.

—ST. FRANCIS XAVIER

XEROX'S RULE: Xerox makes rapid reproductions of human error—perfectly.

YEATS'S 90–90 RULE OF PROJECT SCHEDULING: The first 90 percent of a task consumes 90 percent of the time allotted; the last 10 percent consumes the other 90 percent.

YOUNG'S THEORY OF BUSINESS SECURITY: It is not the crook in modern business that we fear, but the honest man who does not know what he is doing.

—OWEN D. YOUNG

ZANGWILL'S ARCHAEOLOGICAL PRINCIPLE: All towns are built on their dead past, for earth's crust renews itself as incessantly as our own skin.

—ISRAEL ZANGWILL

ZANGWILL'S LAW: Everything changes but change.

—ISRAEL ZANGWILL

ZANGWILL'S RULE: Every dogma has its day, but ideals are eternal.

—ISRAEL ZANGWILL

ZANGWILL'S THEORY OF LITERARY INSIGHT: In the literature of an age the things that are understood are exactly the things that are not written down, and thus the things that are written down are the things that are not understood.

—ISRAEL ZANGWILL

ZEND'S POSTULATE: There are too many people, and too few human beings.

—ROBERT ZEND

ZEND'S PHILOSOPHY: Being a philosopher, I have a problem for every solution.

—ROBERT ZEND

ZEUXIS'S LAW OF PREDICTABLE OUTCOMES: Criticism comes easier than craftsmanship.

—ZEUXIS

ZITTLER'S RULE FOR KICKING THE HABIT: The only way to stop smoking is to just stop—no ifs, ands, or butts.

ZYMURGY'S LAW OF EVOLVING SYSTEMS DYNAMICS: Once you open a can of worms, the only way to recan them is to use a larger can.

References

1. Sheridan Morley, *Oscar Wilde*. New York: Holt, Rinehart and Winston, 1977.

   Alvin Redman, ed., *The Wit and Humor of Oscar Wilde*. New York: Dover Publications, Inc., 1959.

2. Richard Armour, *It All Started with Columbus*. New York: McGraw-Hill Book Company, 1953.

3. ———, *It All Started with Eve*. New York: McGraw-Hill Book Company, 1956.

4. Elbert Hubbard, *A Thousand and One Epigrams*, selected from the writings of Elbert Hubbard. East Aurora, N.Y.: Roycroft Press, 1911.

5. H. J. Eysenck, "The Effects of Psychotherapy: An Evaluation," *Journal of Consulting Psychology* (1952), 16:319–24.

6. E. E. Levitt, "The Results of Psychotherapy with Children: An Evaluation," *Journal of Consulting Psychology* (1957), 21:189–96.

7. W. McCord and J. McCord, *Origins of Crime: A New Evaluation of the Cambridge-Somerville Youth Study*. New York: Columbia University Press, 1959.

8. Waldo R. Browne, ed., *Barnum's Own Story*. New York: Viking, 1927.

Joseph Bryan, *The World's Greatest Showman*. New York: Random House, 1956.

Helen Frances Wells, *Barnum, Showman of America*. New York: David McKay Company, 1957.

9. Jean Nohain and F. Caradec, *Le Petomane*. London: Souvenir Press Ltd., 1967.

10. Joseph Heller, *Catch-22*. New York: Simon and Schuster, 1961.

11. Rama Sinha, *3 Jeers for Bureaucracy*. New Delhi, India: Sangam Books (Orient Longman Ltd.), 1978.

12. Addison Steele, *Upward Nobility, How to Win the Rat Race Without Becoming a Rat*. New York: Times Books, 1978.

13. David Wallechinsky, Irving Wallace, and Amy Wallace, *The Book of Lists*. New York: William Morrow and Company, Inc., 1977.

14. *The CoEvolution Quarterly*. Box 428, Sausalito, California 94965.

15. Wallace Reyburn, *Flushed with Pride: The Story of Thomas Crapper*. Englewood Cliffs, N.J.: Prentice-Hall, Inc., 1971.

16. Paul Tabori, *The Natural Science of Stupidity*. Radnor, Pa.: Chilton Book Company, 1959.

17. Robert N. Kharasch, *The Institutional Imperative: How to Understand the United States Government and Other Bulky Objects*. New York: Charterhouse Books, 1973.

18. Donald G. Smith, *How to Cure Yourself of Positive Thinking*. Miami, Fla.: E. A. Seemann Publishing, Inc., 1976.

19. C. Northcote Parkinson, *Parkinson's Law, or the Pur-*

suit of Progress. Boston: Houghton Mifflin Company, 1957.

20. Laurence J. Peter, *The Peter Principle.* New York: William Morrow and Company, Inc., 1969.

THE BODY BOOK
By Julius Fast

PRICE: $2.25   T51678
CATEGORY: Non-Fiction

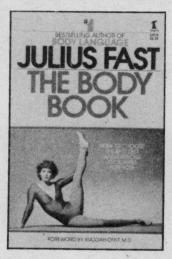

A PERSONALIZED HEALTH PROGRAM!

The bestselling author of BODY LANGUAGE and BODY POLITICS now presents a guide to total health. THE BODY BOOK will help you navigate through the endless maze of diets and exercises to choose the correct—and safest—program for you. Included are tests for fitness, how to improve your total self-image, and how to develop a healthy mind for your new healthy body!